LEARNING
THE PROCESS!

I0009158

HELLO AND WELCOME, you have taken the first step to improving in the design process and improving your graphic design skills. I created this book to help designers learn more about the design process and dive a little further into the world of Photoshop. We'll start by learning where to start, learning about the basics, learning your way, where to find the right tutorials, where to find the right tools and references, but also what you can look forward to...

We will then take a deeper look into the Complete Design Process which includes; your tools of your trade, color balance and manipulation, color symmetry, typography and fonts, where to find usable fonts, where to download fonts, font distribution and balance, image enhancement, image editing, image placement, print ready files...

Before we dive in let's take a minute sit back and relax. Open up your mind to new knowledge and it will be greatly received. First before we dive in, you have to take a minute to realize, what goes into the Graphic Design Process exactly? Knowing this is the first step because you need to know exactly what your goal is.

You can not just start painting, without first knowing what your aim is, same thing goes for the Graphic Design Process. We'll take a deeper look into Learning about Photoshop and the Design Process. This is an in-depth analysis that will help guide you to the right web sites, resources and programs that are made to help you in the design process.

With unlimited resources in an ever-changing field of design, most of these web sites stay up to date with the latest Tutorials and Information. Since most of them are usually free, you are able to grow at your pace and learn the way that best suits you.

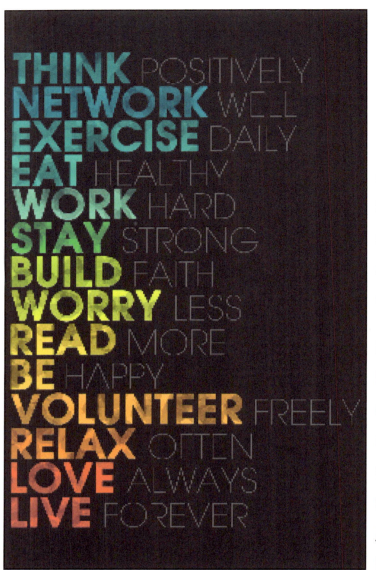

KNOWLEDGE, is power and you can always use it to your advantage. When learning the process of design, you are using your creative mind to come up with some amazing design's. Designing is also about allowing yourself to be able to intake certain knowledge and apply it to what you know. Concentrate on this concept when you are reading this e-book and it will help you along the way.

It's an easy formality to go off what's in your head, but if you know the process and can apply this, you can do a lot in the design world. So keep an open mind when you are learning about what goes into the process of design, this includes learning new tricks and techniques, applying new method's or just trying to find new element's to design with. Follow these step's and they won't let you down.

KNOWLEDGE
IS POWER!

It help's us in our every day lives and because of this we learn new thing's everyday. Use this knowledge to your advantage and learn what you can, while you can. Not only will this help you in the Design Process, but it will help you think more creatively!

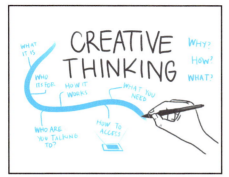

1 CREATIVE MIND AT WORK...

A view into the creative mind at work. Before we dive in, we take a look at some creative thinking and what to think about when your designing. You have the creative mind, it's your ability to use it what ultimately comes into play...

2 THE PROCESS OF LEARNING...

Learning is key to the Design Process. Here we'll talk about the learning process a little, and where you can start. Learn what you can use to help you learn new techniques and lessons, but also new ways to mix and match elements...

3 THE DESIGN PROCESS...

The main focus of the e-book, here we will talk about the complete design process, what you can do and how you can use what you learn. Learning this process helps you expand your creativity and add to your ability...

4 UNDERSTANDING PHOTOSHOP'S ABILITIES...

Who doesn't love having a little more info or incite. Here we take a look at Photoshop and it's incredible elements, effects and tools available to us. We dive in a little about the basics of Photoshop so you can get an easier understanding of what your working with...

5 THE TOOLS OF THE TRADE...

We continue our talks about Photoshop's Capabilities in the design process and take you through some of the amazing ways that Photoshop can help you with your design...

6 THE POWER OF IMAGES...

In this chapter we discuss all about images, where to find them and which ones to use. We also discuss Image Placement and using space wisely; so your creative design has symmetry and balance...

7 TWENTY ONE AWESOME TIPS...

Last but not least, I give you an ultimate compilation of 21 tip's that are created to give you an edge over your creative side....

Creative thinking can sometimes seem to be a missing commodity. Although you see many designs and illustrations out there, there have not been to many individual decisions in the creative process. These days groups of designers take in part the creative side, and then work out what they seem to perceive to be their objective. They take concepts and ideas just like me and you, and turn them into sell able profits.

CREATIVE THINKING CAN GO A LONG WAY!

Some companies even seem to have pre-made templates, so their is not much to designing anymore by yourself. "Most people think they are Graphic Designers themselves, they are horribly mistaken, unfortunately it's far and in-between." This statement couldn't be any more true. Many people out therer sit down and automatically think that they are designers. It doesn't quite happen that way. It takes some time to be a designer, and to learn the abilities and capabilities of all the design programs out there. Whether you try to manage them all or focus on just a few, to get to be good at what you do, takes time and practice. In the graphic design field, creative thinking is a great asset to have.

That's where creative thinking comes into play. Creative thinking is all about thinking about the problem and creating a solution to that problem, sometimes from a fresh new perspective. Everyone is creative in there own right, it's just how they harness that creativity that makes each one stand out. Your ability to create mind blowing graphics and concepts all leads up to the time and effort you put into your creative designs. Putting new perspectives on old design concepts, can make you see more ideas as they come along.

Let's look at creative thinking and your ability to adapt and create just from your ideas and concepts. When you think about creative thinking, although you might think solutions, in the design world the first thing that stands out to you is IMAGINATION, however you

CREATIVE MIND!

Check out this awesome example of the creative mind at work. This prime example shows you an artistic view of how your brain may process your logic and creative sides. This awesome image shows the split of contemplation when it comes to design.

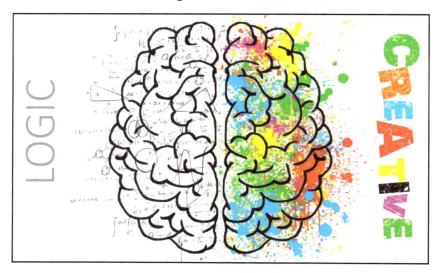

want to look at it, this one mental element is seen as the strategic move to all creative thinking. New valuable lessons can be learned from exploring your creativity side and in the design world, new fresh perspectives can go a long way.

Without our imagination's, we technically have nothing, no ideas, no concepts, no thoughts, therefore Imagination plays a huge role in the design process. Knowing and seeing what your goal or aim is, will eliminate the design process in half, but will help you learn new ways to design.

Thinking creatively, I don't know if that's even a word, but doing it helps you develop solutions to

your problems with a fresh new perspective on original artwork or creating new artwork from scratch. Being creative also allows you to go against the norm, using past and previous experiences.

Looking at these previous experiences, will help your imagination create and think of new concepts and ideas. Sometimes self-diversity can play a huge role, whether you are looking to stand out at work or just looking to stand out amongst other designers, being creative gives you this ability.

The benefits of being creative are extremely beneficial because it allows you to try out new ideas and concepts, without having to worry about impressions. Please note that you will have to take a lot of criticism in the design field, but I promise you, it's all worth it in the end.

Lets get back to thinking creatively and using your creative mind to create some amazing graphics. Someone once said; "Creativity is a phenomenon whereby something new and somehow valuable is formed." Listen to this statement as it has a lot of common sense to it.

CREATIVE THINKING & IDEAS!

As I stated before, there hasn't been much originality or creativeness in today's design field. A lot of designs are based off of previous or past designs, which hinder's us from our abilities and stops us from adding our own originality to the design. This limits your capabilities and abilities.

When you think about something and develop a solid plan, you are not sticking with the typical solution, you are creating a new unorthodox solution, that are not based on past traditional solutions. Now that you see the creative side of the design process, you can understand what it entails and you can use it to your advantage.

In the near future, being a commodity might come in handy, college students today are learning new technology on a daily basis. Being able to creatively think about what your goal is will help you breakdown piece by piece what you are trying to accomplish.

Think of it as having a complicated problem that you are trying to solve and you simply lay out all the ideas and find the solution that works best.

What can kill you in the process is doubt, do not doubt what you are aiming to achieve because one little doubt can offset your entire creative thinking process. This forces you to start the process all over again, but this can be a blessing sometimes, if it does seem to happen.

Being able to creatively think about what your goal is will help you breakdown piece by piece what you are trying to accomplish. Think of it as having a complicated problem that you are trying to solve and you simply lay out all the ideas and find the solution that works best.

What can kill you in the process is doubt, do not doubt what you are aiming to achieve because one little doubt can offset your entire creative thinking process. This forces you to start the process all over again, but this can be a blessing sometimes, if it does seem to happen. ▶

CREATING THE UNCREATABLE!

I've learned in my time that what you aim to design can sometimes come across as something totally new and innovative, although not totally meant to be. As you aim to create new and amazing graphics, you learn new ways of designing and come across things that you may have not even considered.

This is what I love about designing, every time you learn something and think of new ideas or concepts, you create things that seem to be uncreatable.

I am sure you have seen some of the incredible Photoshop images out there, they all started with an idea and concept. Focus on the design process with creative thinking, it literally can save your life. ▶

QUICK TIPS FOR CREATIVE THINKING!

1 **IMAGINE** - your own imagination is your key to success. Using it allows you the capability of learning new and exciting trends and designs. You can imagine new different concepts and ideas off of old or original artwork. Your always going to be thinking and creating new ideas.

2 **BREAKDOWN** your ideas and concepts for your artwork. This breakdown will ultimately help you in the long run. Taking a step back and looking at the bigger picture will allow you to use your creative thinking to ultimately come up with new ideas and concepts.

3 **DESIGN** - now is the time to put your ideas to the canvas. Here is where you will be putting together your ideas and concepts for your designs. Thinking about your placement, the entire look of your design, feel of your design, and what you want to your center point.

4 **CREATE** - easy concept, very hard to accomplish. You have already thought about your design, you know what you want to do and how, now it's just a matter of putting it all together. Your creative mind is now working full throttle, so come up with different concepts before engaging.

Creativity is the ability to come up with exciting new ideas and concepts and implement these into your designs. You don't have to be an artist to be a creative thinker.

Some people are naturally more creative than others, but creative thinking can be strengthened with time and practice. Thinking creatively bring's a fresh and unorthodox perspective to your designs.

Coming up with ideas no one has ever seen before may seem like a bit of a challenge, but most graphic designers are up for that challenge and take it head on. Let's take a dive into another part of your own creative thinking process and let's talk about implementation and the process of implementing elements with your images.

IMPLEMENTATION

Another element of creative thinking is implementation. What course are you going to take to figure out the solution and what abilities do you have to provide that solution. You have to remember creative thinking involves there ability to perceive patterns or concepts that are not obvious.

One thing I like about creative thinking is the ability to let go of your preconceived assumptions. This is sometimes a hindrance on your designs and could cause delay and hesitation.

If you have ever heard the term "Writer's Block," you'll know what I am referring too. Your ability to keep an open-mind allows you to see things in new ways that no one else can.

Look at how an artist create's their painting, they implement their own experiences and feelings into it, you can do the same thing here, but your using Photoshop as your canvas. What I like about the ability to be creative, is knowing that you are looking at things in a different way.

There is technically no limit to ways there are of thinking creatively, since creative thinking is often implementing unorganized and unpredictable solutions. You take a new view into solving problems, these views included look at things from several perspectives, then implementing the plan that you think fits best. Some may be wrong, but that's what helps you learn. ▶

DESIGN & CREATIVE THINKING...

After creative implementation there is the design process of creative thinking and thinking creatively. You may think to yourself, design process? Yes, the

design process. What I mean is here is where all your ideas and concepts come together. Here you'll be thinking about placement, look of your design, feel of your design, and what message you are trying to get across.

Your creative message relays what you are feeling. Like we have discussed before some designs are created off of self experience and emotional experience. The creative thought that goes into them is purely off of life experience, this experience alone can project years of self expression and self learning. Creative thinking can sometimes have an emotional factor to it, not all designs will have it, but some will.

Since you are designing on pure creativity, this allows you to gather up your ideas and concepts, think about what you want to design and then put the plan in action.

When you think about something and develop a solid plan, you are not sticking with the typical solution, you are creating a new unorthodox solution, that are not based on past traditional solutions. Now that you see the creative side of the design process, you can understand what it entails and you can use it to your advantage.

In the near future, being a commodity might come in handy, college students today are learning new technology on a daily basis. ▶

CREATIVE MIND AT WORK!

Think before you design. You are the designer, not anyone else. Ignore the voices and listen to your creative mind, this will help you in the long run.

I can never express this enough with my clients and customers, you are the designer and not anyone else. A lot of people will be making suggestions of what to do and not to do, SURE, you can take their advice, but always remember that you are the designer and you ultimately decide what you are aiming to design...

Through all the ideas and concepts that you may come across you are always going to be able to learn new and innovative ways to designing. You can even use your creative thinking in real life, and really should. This allows you to perceive new information that you can use to make decisions on new problems. As we discussed before one main part of creative thinking is looking at your designs with a fresh perspective, then taking this perspective and applying it to your everyday thoughts.

Use your mind, that is the best part of creative thinking. As the headline says this is your Creative Mind At Work, you are the artist and it's up to you to create your masterpiece. Learning new techniques and new information is what allows you to be a creative thinker, using this book will help you attain new information and knowledge that can become very helpful and inspire you to think outside the box.

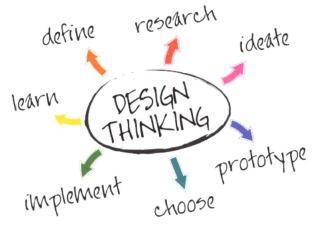

"IMAGINATION IS MORE IMPORTANT THAN KNOWLEDGE"

CREATING your masterpiece is just a step away. There are plenty of creative thinking ways that can go into your decision's. What's best to do is analyze everything you can about the problem or design, then apply what solutions you think works best. This may not seem to apply in the design world, but it's an element that plays an exceptional role. Making informed judgements help's you find the right mix of fonts and colors to use in your designs. You find the right balance and symmetry so your design flows and has a symmetrical balance. Creative thinking and critical thinking can be a major part of the Design Process and the way you mix elements.

CREATIVE THINKING IN DESIGN!

I might make it seem an easy thing to do, but in reality creative thinking is an important process. Now quickly becoming an invaluable skill, if you can develop this skill you become a useful creative thinker amongst your peers. You'll be able to look at problems with a fresh perspective, using new technology, new information, new programs and new details to figure out well informed solutions.

WHY TALK ABOUT CREATIVE THINKING?

This might seem like something that has nothing to do with design, but believe me it does. If I can drill anything into your mind, is that being able to creatively think about your problems allows you to analyze them with a more relaxed attitude, more calmer approach and more calmer state.

Taking a more unethical approach to design allows you to utilize all you capabilities. Why rush something that you can take your time with and still finish on time. Your unorthodox approach to creative thinking is what keeps you ahead of the game and able to learn new techniques your way. ▶

LEARNING, is a very important factor when it comes to design. When it comes to designing, learn the process of design your way. Focus on what you do best. If you are good at photo-editing; perfect that, if your good at designing from scratch; perfect that. Stick to what you want to learn and do because in the end it will all come down to you.

What I love about program's like Photoshop, is that Photoshop is built to allow you to learn at your pace, as in the old words, practice makes perfect. Learning your way allows you to develop new techniques, learn how to manipulate images and fonts,

THE POWER OF
LEARNING!

It help's to learn everything you can and knowledge is power, so let's take a step by stpe approach to The Process Of Learning, and how you can use it to your advantage.

but ultimately help you become a better Graphic Designer. There are all several types of elements and attributes that go into a good design.

Creative Learning

USE LESSONS TO THERE FULLEST!

It's up to you to focus on how to use these elements and learn everything you can about these elements. Your main goal of learning is to focus on your creative ideas and concepts, this is what designing is all about. Your taking elements and providing a clear solution to the problem, as seen through creativity.

You want to learn how to create eye-catching detail orientated designs, and studying and learning lessons can help you. Designing takes time and practice, but as you sit down and design, you come up with new ideas all the time. Perfecting these elements helps you stay focused on the 3 main disciplines of design; Balance, Contrast and Hierarchy.

You will soon realize as you start to learn all about Photoshop and the design process, that there are several elements and techniques that goes into designing. It's your job to focus on what you know and learn what you can do, this will allow you to learn new steps and techniques along the way.

PERFECT WHAT YOU KNOW!

Remember that Graphic Design is the process of taking ideas, concepts, elements and putting them all together using your mind to create a new inspiring piece of artwork.

With the invaluable skill of creative thinking slowly dying, it's up to you to learn new ways. Learning new ways to create or manipulate designs or artwork allows you to use all your capabilities. ▶

THINK before you design. This may seem simple, and it technically is, but it plays a huge role in the design process. We have already talked about creative thinking, and how they go hand in hand. Will the ability to learn new techniques and concepts you are able to come up with new ideas that are outside the box, but create value to your artwork. Since it's a creative piece, you are the painter and you are the artist, so there will always be thoughts roaming around in your head. It's up to you to how much you want to learn about your profession.

KNOWING IS HALF THE BATTLE!

As in the old saying, Knowledge is power, learning the basics of Photoshop or any design program, provides you with the know how and enhances a whole new world of creativity. There are so many elements that go into a design, knowing the basics , allows you to use your creativity to think before you act. With alignment, repetition, balance, and the power of color, it's good to know what abilities you have at your disposal.

TURNING NOTHING INTO SOMETHING!

This is not an easy thing to do, but with Photoshop and it's incredible abilities, they'll help you cut the time in half. In learning the basics with Photoshop, you will find that Photoshop has gone all out and provides you with the ultimate starter's guide. With new tools, special effect's and capabilities, they provide you an excellent canvas to learn and apply your knowledge, even if you have the lower version.

It is now even easier to learn how to enhance and edit photos, create color manipulation, but also create eye-catching artwork. ▶

STUDY NEW IDEAS & TECHNIQUES!

The Learning Process can contain numerous varieties of ways to learn new and fresh information. Knowledge is power so too study this knowledge through and through will help you become a better designer. Photoshop doesn't limit you to what you can learn, and it's all up to you to learn what you want. You can pick and choose certain techniques or go for the bang and learn as much as you can, like I said it's totally up to you.

You have already taken the first step with this book you are reading. Here I will teach you on the art of learning, where to start and how to gain from what you already know. You've heard the term of study group, you can use the same logic here. Take the time to learn all you can about new elements and old elements. With Photoshop, you will discover that all new elements are based off past and previous element's.

These element's tend to change in time, whether they are made better or newly created, studying them can really enhance your capabilities and abilities to create better emphasis in your design's.

Even taking an hour or two a day to look at new elements can open your eyes to new information, concepts and ideas.

WHERE TO GET STARTED!

I know you might be asking, shouldn't this be at the beginning. No. Let me explain why. I wrote this book to take you step by step, process by process, but through the entire and complete design process.

I want you to be thinking about these concepts and ideas as we go along and get further into our discussion about the design process.

From here we will get deeper into the design process and learn all about the creative thinking that goes into the design process. We'll learn about the main 3 main principals that will always come into play, which if you may not know, you will soon.

In the Learning The Design Process it is always good to start with the basics of Photoshop & The Design process, learning the basics helps you to accept and intake new information that you may have not known or thought of, remember you're the creative thinker. ▶

TUTORIALS ARE MADE FOR YOU!

Hundreds of tutorials are uploaded daily, these are tutorials that are made for you. You can view these tutorials and lessons anytime and technically anywhere. I added four of the main web sites up above, these web sites will help you learn some of the basics, but also offer's more advanced tutorials for the expert and intermediate designers.

Learn as much as you can from tutorials. Don't think you ever to old to learn new things, because you are not. Learning new things is what enhances our knowledge and allows us the ability to create new and inspiring things. Use these to your advantage to keep you ahead of your peers and ahead of the game.

As an ever-changing world, new aspects and techniques of design can be seen on a daily basis, learning and studying these different aspects of design is what gaining new knowledge and learning is all about. Take the time to sit down and learn these at your pace. Don't rush to learn something new because this will ultimately keep you from skipping step's and getting lost if you miss a step.

Since these tutorial's are available 24/7, you are never limited to a time frame. You can easily learn at your time and pace and digest every new technique that can be learned. Also each web site has different lessons, so never stick to one site. ▶

GOOD TUTORIAL'S TO LEARN FROM!

There are several web sites provided for you that can help you with tutorials. These excellent Photoshop web sites contain numerous videos and tutorials, that will allow you to learn Photoshop your way.

www.tutorialized.com
www.photoshoptutorials.ws
www.photoshopessentials.com
www.phlearn.com/free-tutorials/
www.photoshopcafe.com/tutorials
www.phlearn.com/photoshop-tutorial's.com

Take a look at some of the web site's above. These very easy-to-use web sites provide free resources and tutorials for you to be able to learn your way and at your pace. Learn from these web sites and tutorial's, and don't worry because new lessons and tutorial's are uploaded daily. ▶

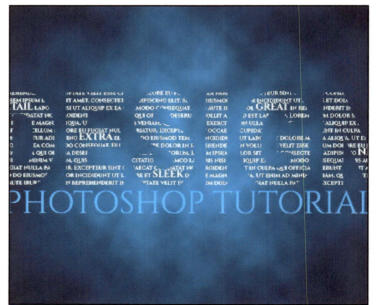

TUTORIALS HELP CREATE IDEAS!

As you evolve in the design world, you are always learning and changing to adapt to new perspectives, like it is often said, no two design's are ever going to be the same. Expanding your horizons to new heights is always what dreaming big is all about. Without dreaming big, we are stuck to the simple minds of no concept and imagination.

With the help of tutorial's and lesson's you are able to use your imagination and not limit yourselves to the simple concepts, you create new and exciting ideas to run with. Creating these new ideas is what helps you come up with new concepts for design, since this process is ever-changing, you are never limited to what you can create or conceive. ▶

DON'T KILL YOURSELF ON TUTORIALS!

Please listen and do not, I repeat do not, kill yourselves on Tutorials or lessons. A lot of things can go into one simple lesson or tutorial, but don't beat yourself up if you are not getting it. People tend to get mad if they don't understand a concept, and getting mad, will hinder you from learning. Take your time, if you don't understand something take a break and then come back with a fresh new attack. ▶

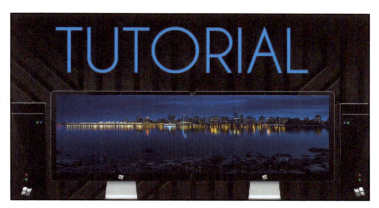

BEFORE WE DIVE IN, REMEMBER THESE QUICK LEARNING TIPS!

1 **STUDY** - take the time to look at new elements of design. Study new trends, styles and techniques. Doing this will not only enhance your creativity, but in the end will give you a new perspective to work from. As a creative thinker, new ideas come to us all the time.

2 **ANALYZE** - your ideas and concepts for your artwork. Taking a step back to look at the bigger picture will allow you to use your creative thinking to ultimately come up with the concept you want to go with. When concept is such a key feature, it's hard to dive in without any direction.

3 **LEARN** - now is the time to learn what you can and while you can. Photoshop has plenty of tutorials, designs and lessons easily available for you to learn and study. You don't have to learn every detail, but easily knowing what you can do and can't do will help in the long run.

4 **IMPLEMENT** - what you have learned and studied. You know what you have to do and what you have to accomplish, now it's just a matter of taking that simple knowledge and applying it to your creative design or artwork. In doing so new and interesting strategies comes into play.

DESIGNING, is a very important factor when it comes to creativity. When it comes to designing, learning the process of design can go a long way. Focus on what you do best. If you are good at photo-editing; perfect that, if your good at designing from scratch; perfect that. Stick to what you know how to do and learn how to perfect it.

In this section is it all about Design and what goes into the thought process when were designing. We will look at the Power Of Contrast and how it play's a very important role. How Balance can easily offset and create imbalance within your design, but also we will learn about the Power Of Color, and how you can use it to your advantage. Since Color is one of your main element's, it is good to learn everything you can about it. Like the great saying goes, knowledge is the key to power, or at

THE POWER OF
DESIGN!

Take a step by step look at The Process of Design and what goes into it. We will dive into the Power Of Contrast, the Power of Perfect Balance and the Power of Color.

least I hope so. Before we dive into them though, we will talk a little about the Design Process and what goes into the beginning stages. A lot claim that there are six or seven golden rules to design, but it ultimately comes down to how you want to create your masterpiece. These basic rules can help you stay organized by laying a solid foundation when you get started.

Understanding the direction of the design can be easier when you are starting from scratch. Working one-on-one with your customer or client can easily send you in the direction, with a satisfying ending result. Use this time wisely to study your customer's needs, but also what their ultimate advertisement goal is and who there trying to reach for an audience.

CREATIVE BRIEF OF DESIGN!

RESEARCH & BRAINSTORM!

All creative processes start somewhere and with design, your creative process starts with The Creative Brief. The Creative Brief is all about you and the client or customer, what their aim is and what they would like to see as the end result. Understanding the client's needs, goals, mission and audience is what will help you in your design process. The creative brief will help you and your client get on the same page to figure out what they want and need out of the design.

Now it's time to take what you have learned in your Creative Brief and think about how to apply it to your design.

Since you have done the research and have a good direction to go, you can ultimately start planning and researching for your design. You know what the client's goal's are, now it's time for you to sit down sit down and start planning out your design. Brainstorm different ideas and concepts so you can come up with the ultimate design. Also don't forget to share these ideas with your client, because you are constantly changing and coming up with ideas, once one click's, it's good to be on the same page with your client.

There's tons of free samples that are provided easily by online wallpaper's, some of these images used are from them. You can take these ideas and concepts and spin them in a new way. Take ideas from them and inspire new ones. ▶

CREATING YOUR CONCEPTS!

Now that you have done the research and are ready to put ideas to paper, you can lay out your concept's and start sketching. This is where your creative mind starts to work. Make sure that for your first round of concepts, stick with sketching your ideas out on paper, this can help tremendously since ideas and concept's are ever-changing.

You and your client are on the same page, it's time to go to work; so think creatively. Lay out your concepts and place them in a way that is pleasing to you, doing this helps you focus on your focal point.

Since their is a goal to the design, creating a center Focal Point helps you focus the direction and perception of the design. Also with this center focal point, it allows your viewer or reader focus on what is of importance and what is not. This is beneficial for your client because it gives them the ability to showcase what is important to their customers. Knowing the audience your client or customer is trying to attract will allow you to better focus on the end game.

You don't have to be an amazing artist to draw up your concept's. A simple explanation of what you are trying to achieve can be easily drawn in a simple fashion. If you are an amazing artist, well then keep up the good work, but in all reality a simple sketch of what you aim is, should be just fine.

Take this time to share your concepts with your client, since it's their decision of what you are trying to achieve, they can help in the direction process. It's easier to know where you are going, then to just go off what you think is the right path, but this is where all that comes into play.

You are drawing out your concept's so you can easily arranged them in a balanced manner, which instantly attracts your viewer's eyes, drawing them into your center focal point. ▶

DESIGNS GOT TO BE REFINED!

The next processes you will run into in the design process will be the Revision and the Refined Stages. Although they might seem the same, they have there differences. You will meet with your client to edit and change different elements in your design, but also here is where you will start putting together your creative design together on your computer.

You are now taking your concept's and ideas and creating a unique artwork that helps your client achieve their goal. This is also where our creative side comes further into play because we are creating in a way to add depth and appeal to a design that started from scratch. You will spend most of your time in the creation phase, but be aware that if done incorrectly, your time will be here. ▶

REVISIONS ARE ALL PART OF IT!

When it comes to revisions, and getting feedback, remember that you are the professional that is getting hired to do this work, so feedback is necessary. A lot of designer's will get annoyed to quickly and become overwhelmed with their work, leaving the design to be unfinished.

Think of it at criticism, you can take it and do what you want with it, or you can let it tear you up from the inside. Be the professional and listen to feedback, because it's really the end design that everyone is aiming to achieve. Don't forget about the Creative Brief, remember that you created the design with a specific goal in mind.

One thing good about Revision's is that you can collaborate what each other is feeling about the design, this collaboration can help you better understand the end result. Since you have already been back and forth with your client, most Revisions will come easily, and not add to much confusion.

YOUR DONE, ITS FINAL!

After your revisions have been approved, it's time to deliver the final design. Use everything you have learned and apply it in a pleasant appealing way that impresses your client or customer. Your ultimate goal is to achieve the perfect balance between what your client wanted and what the ultimate goal was.

Though getting these two to coincide can be a bit tricky, if you took the right step's and followed the process of design, you should come out just fine, and be able to create some amazing design's..

Following the right steps can help you along your way, but you don't necessarily have to follow these steps in order. Since we are all unique in our own right, no two designs will ever be the same. ▶

BEFORE WE DIVE IN, LETS TAKE A LOOK AT WHAT WE WILL DISCUSS!

1 CONTRAST - this plays a big role in the process of design. It's what allows you to create depth and intensity to your elements. There are four main principals to Contrast and we will discuss how they mix.

2 BALANCE - You will learn more about balance in design and the key role it plays. As in life, having balance allows you to live a healthy and stable life, such is needed in design. Symmetrical Balance is key.

3 TYPE - Typography is the ultimate tool to your creativity. With typography you can easily add interest to your design. Your text can be displayed in several ways, so type plays a pivotal role in the design process.

4 COLOR - the ultimate element tool to help you in design, Color add's visual appeal to your design. Because we are quickly are drawn to color, it can be easily used to create contrast between your elements.

**C**ONTRAST. In learning the basics in the design process, you will learn a tremendous amount about the 3 main principals of creative design. These 3 main principal's are Contrast, Balance and Color. They are known as the main 3 principal's because they have the most use, but are also known as the simple rules and basic principal's to follow.

MAKING YOUR DESIGN INTERESTING!

First we will look at the Principal Of Contrast and learn about what Contrast can entail. Contrast plays a major roll in any creative design or creative artwork.

What is Contrast you might ask? Contrast refers to the simple process of placing different or opposite elements in your design so they create a visual interest. Adding opposite elements in your creative designs helps add interest to your design and showcases what's important to the viewer. Contrast has the keen sense to make your creative design more interesting by helping draw out the main elements of your concept. In this simple process you are taking different elements, some more important then others and placing them in a way that can catch your viewer's attention. You can think of it like having an event. You have done the prep work and have everything ready for the event, now it's just a matter of time of putting the show together and focusing on showcasing the main focal point.

The simple process of adding Contrast to your creative artwork can range from many things. As an emphasizer, you are able to use a number of elements to help focus on the message at hand, it is said that our eyes like Contrast.

Your focusing on creating an art piece that not only can be appealing, but can also be organized but have a symmetrical balance to it. With Contrast you are able to mix and match different tones and elements to get the look and feel that you ultimately aim for in the end.

As in any process, there is a hierarchy, but with Contrast you are able to easily establish the hierarchy, to use and maintain visual interest. ▶

CONTRAST & ELEMENT PLACEMENT

The one main thing about Contrast is that you are taking opposite elements and placing them n a way that helps create visual interest. Using Contrast can help you create something that is exciting and interesting, seeing that your job is to create something that has visual interest with a bit of excitement and drama.

A contrast is achieved not only by using the right color combination use, but also with the help of color's, fonts, textures and shapes. You have to choose the right method for every creative art design you make. We will discuss the top four methods next, after we finish our discussion here.

Contrast helps organize your design and establish a hierarchy, which simply shows which parts of your design are more important then other's. Using the ability of Contrast with different elements can enhance your chance to keep the hierarchy intact, but also create good visual interest to your designs. You want to remember this information when you are designing with Contrast. As it is often said that to much can cause your design to be overdone, losing focus, so you have to find your perfect balance.

As I stated before, Contrast allows you the ability to use several elements with your design to help create the right Contrast between your elements. Contrast should always be placed in a balanced way, this is because it is emphasizing the focal point of your design and good use of Contrast adds visual interest.

A simple design where everything is the same size, shape or color is going to look boring, but with the addition of contrast you can add an exciting and visual interest.

Unfortunately, there's no magic formula or secret's for Contrast, the process often happen's sub-consciously as you are putting together your design concept. Contrast is a design element that anyone can use to organize and add visual interest to their design projects. ▶

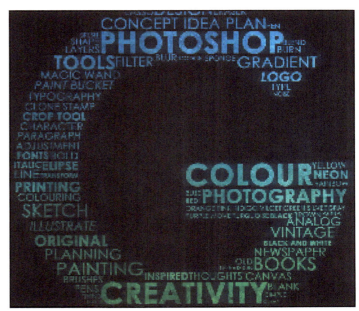

TOTAL OPPOSITES ATTRACT!

When thinking about placing opposite elements together keep in mind that opposites attract. In general, you're taking separate elements and presenting them in a manner that's appealing to your viewer. Contrast can be used to create variety, emphasis, dominance, balance, hierarchy, interest and help achieve your design goals.

But if not placed or used right, you can totally throw off your design, making it unappealing to your viewer. You have to find the right balance between these elements to blend them in the right way, since placement is key, try starting from a center point and go from there. This Center Point will help you focus on what is of interest and what is not, since each design has their own ultimate goal, it's up to you to decide on how these opposite elements will help attract your viewer when placed right.

You'll here this often when it comes to Asymmetrical Balance, because this is a form of Balanced that is used when different elements are offset from each other. Architect's tend to capitalize on this Balance theory because it allows them to use a different sense of balance when it comes to designing. Since architecture is often seen as an expression of the architect or the owner, they are not limited to the standard square or rectangle design format.

Concentrate on using the right elements to blend and mix, so these elements won't offset your design and will keep it balanced. Take turns placing different images and elements to see how they contrast with each other, this will help you get a jist of what elements go together and what elements do not go together..

EMPHASIS ON CONTRAST!

I am sure you have heard the saying, put emphasis on it, which in turn, basically means explain the situation or show a balanced visual presentation to showcase what you are talking about. This is what you get with Contrast, you are able to use this design tool to create the emphasis on what your goal is.

Think about the process before you start to design. Consider what you are aiming for, what's going to give you that visual interest, but help keep your design symmetrically balanced. The good thing about Photoshop is that they allow you to add emphasis to your design with so many different elements and options. You are not limited to the amount of Contrast you can add, but keep in mind you need to be able to keep each element symmetrically balanced.

Some of the main design elements used to create Contrast with emphasis is Color and Texture. Since both can easily add emphasis to your design, these are the most commonly used methods of Contrast.

You are not limited there though, cause with these methods comes a tremendous amount of options. In the Design process, with color blending, color mixtures and textures, you can constantly create emphasis in your designs. ▶

Contrast Elements!

SIZE -- *You will use different elements in size contrast. Small vs large, weight vs thickness.*

TYPE -- *A huge element, size, color, weight, small, large, here you will try to use opposites to attract.*

COLOR -- *Luckily you have an abundance of different color options to work with, being this is one serious element.*

SHAPES -- *The size and look can sometimes be overdone, so use various shapes wisely when you are trying to create contrast with them.*

TEXTURES -- *A favorite to designers, this can add depth and a new look and feel to your design.*

IMAGES -- *Using different images can really help offset your design. Seeing that images range in a variety of sizes, this will help you expendetually.*

DIFFERENCE -- *You want to make sure your contrast is different because the greater the difference, the greater the contrast. Your goal is to make sure the difference is obvious, but not too overdone.*

Use Color and Texture to add interest

SIZE CONTRAST. When it comes to CONTRAST, there are four commonly used methods for creating appealing Contrast. It's hard to just go off scratch, but with these four common methods of Contrast you are able to control your differences. These four common methods used to create differences are size, color, value and type. The method that we will be discussing first is Size Contrast.

USING SIZE FOR CONTRAST!

One of the main methods used to showcase contrast is Size. This can range from similar type to similar images, but also shapes and textures when combining them. The most common use of size contrast you will see is with images and fonts. You'll work with small and large images of the same type, (meaning the same image), but also small and large type.

Take a look at the picture to the left. It's used to showcase the difference in size contrast between font's and images and the hierarchy it shows.

HIERARCHY
LETS THE READER KNOW
WHERE TO LOOK FIRST.

ELEMENT OF DESIGN
CONTRAST

The main key to size contrast is making sure there is an obvious difference. Think about it this way, without contrast your reader or viewer doesn't know where to look or what may be of importance. Since their is no direction to the design, there is no interest or appeal to the design.

This can be frustrating to your viewers since when they look at a design, they expect to get the message. if their is no clear message, this can offset your design and uninterest your viewer.

One thing you can focus on with size contrast is using the right type size contrast because this can easily increase your readability. Type can be edited and tampered with in many ways, so using the right type and size can come as a great benefit.

Most headings and sub-headings deal in the use of size contrast. Heading's catch reader's and viewer's eyes and attracts them to the importance of the article or design, making it more readable. ▶

Type Elements!

Size -- You will use different elements in size contrast. Small vs large, weight vs thickness., light vs dark.

Hierarchy -- As you can see in the image to the left, hierarchy can help you place emphasis on what is important and what may not be so important.

Color-- No other element plays a bigger role in your design then Color does. Color can add depth and intensity to a very bland design. Your goal is to make your viewer interested.

MIXING SMALL WITH LARGE!

The one main thing to remember is that Contrast is not equal, one element will be more visibly cynamic then it's opposite. This contrast is what helps catch the reader's eye to what's more immediately visible and what takes presence. Your goal with s ze contrast is to create a sense of visual interest with your design.

Using the right Size Contrast can keep you from going wrong because with Size Contrast using too much can throw off your design and completely destroy your appeal or interest.

Stay focused on using the right amounts of size contrast with your elements and it will allow you to keep balance and harmony. As we discussed before a creative design that has all the same size, color, or shapes, will be dull and boring. You can use Size

Contrast to help you emphasis your ideas and information. Using bigger fonts compared to smaller fonts, can help distinguish between headlines and messages.

You can also use images to help you achieve this goal, because bigger images are always seen before smaller images, but both are needed to get the visual interest that you want. A bigger image beside a smaller image generally indicates that the bigger image is far more important. Your aim is to creative a visual piece where your main objects are distinguishable from other objects and even the background. Sometimes this can be a bit tricky, but with practice and always learning new techniques you should be just fine.

Opposite elements are the easiest way to grasp what Size Contrast is, but when applying size contrast to your design work it's never quite as simple as it seems. As you start to place elements, you get a idea of what you want to do. Go off this idea and it will help guide you along the design process. ▶

THE TEXT IN THIS CONTRAST IS INCREDIBLY
HUGE

SIZE DOES MATTER!

That is right, I am saying size does matter, because it really does. Creating a hierarchy of importance using size contrast is what gives a design its appeal and interest. You are using size elements to help you create organization of your information. You can't just place random sized elements and images thinking they'll get it. You have to place your elements in a way that your message is easily perceived, doing this maintains a healthy balance of harmony.

One thing that is easily recognized in the design world is the use of Size Contrast. As an example, billboards are prime real estate for Size Contrast. The ability to use different sized elements gives depth to their advertisements.

Small fonts and images are used to draw out bigger fonts and images. With the use of Size Contrast they are able to focus the viewers attention and emphasize the information that they want to get across. Since you usually are creating a center point for your viewers to focus on, you can use Size Contrast to help you achieve this goal.

Size Contrast is also one of the main contrast elements used to help you create emphasis in your design, this is because bigger fonts are easily seen before smaller fonts. This is also when hierarchy comes into play because you are using size difference to create a center point. ▶

Hierarchy can help you in Size Contrast because you can use different sizes to display different information. The more important information can get displayed bigger with a higher contrast so it becomes the main focal point of the design, since the smaller elements will be playing the supportive role.

I stress the Center Focal Point because this is ultimately what your design's all comes down to. You are creating a design that with interest and appeal to your viewer, but their has to be some appeal for the viewer to be drawn in to peak that interest and make it something they would like to view. ▶

TYPOGRAPHY & CONTRAST!

If you want to achieve size contrast through typography, you'll often ask which fonts should you use? Fonts can easily very, because there are so many fonts out there and new ones are created daily. If you are limited on font's and what some good font's to download, feel free to go to www.dafont.com. This is an awesome free source for font's are you are limited to a certain amount of download's, you can download just about every one you like and see.

Working with font's can be tricky, but since there is plenty of font's out there and font's made for certain criteria's, you will easily be able to find the right font's to use. The use of font's will allow you to add depth and intensity to your design because it sets an hierarchy and structure. One thing that is awesome with font's is they provide different weighted styles to use to add emphasis to your design. ▶

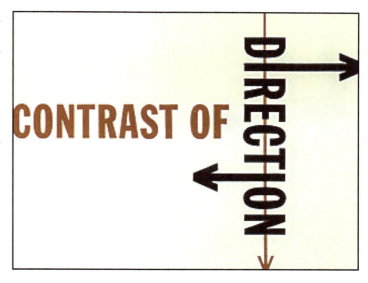

Size Contrast helps your viewer's eyes focus on the direction your design is perceived to go. Since this ultimately gives you the direction your eye's are tended to follow, you can use different Size Contrast to make sure the viewer is following the same path.

From type and weight too color, the use of Size will always come into play, it's up to you to make sure that you use it with the right elements, to help attract your viewer or reader. ▶

contrast your type with **weight**

THIS STATEMENT HAS NO CONTRAST.

This statement has
CONTRAST.

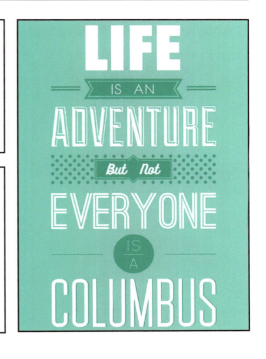

COLOR CONTRAST. IN The second most commonly used form of contrast is, COLOR. Color can be your enemy, but if utilized right can be your best friend. It play's a powerful role in your design and it's how you utilize this power that's left up to you. Think of Color Contrast as a power player, this is due to the fact that your color scheme always comes into play with your design, but the option of having numerous elements to choose from can be your downfall. Color is utilized greatly in design because it is the one element that you can use to catch your reader's or viewer's eyes from a distance. Even though size might play a role in this, it's easier to spot color's, from a distance, then it is to see bigger letters.

A MULTITUDE OF COLOR!

Color Contrast is an element that has to be closely watched and used. When you think about it Color Contrast has many phases to it. Although it is a simple element to use, there is a lot of creativity that goes into picking the right colors to choose. For example, not only are you dealing with you color's matching each other and staying balanced, you are also dealing with color size, color depth, light vs dark, color schemes, color blending, color intensity, but also color weight and distribution. Finding the right colors to blend allows you to create pleasing material, without having the confusion of dealing with mismatched color schemes.

Artist love using Color Contrast because it allows them the ability to create focal points with the ease of just using color. You have seen billboards, they use color as a huge element to keep there information separate. You will see them using this process by using the same color on several elements and then drawing out the main focal element with a different color.

As we dive into Color Contrast you will learn about the six color schemes used to think about color, how you can mix and match certain colors, but also about color temperature, intensity and texture. ▶

Contrast Elements!

Color Wheel -- Your ultimate guide to color is the Color Wheel. With this you are able to mix and match useful color's.

Color Modes -- These are Often referenced as a way of understanding the color's you are using better.

USING THE RIGHT SCHEME!

You have enough color options provided for you to choose from with the excellent Color Wheel, but designer's have taken this a step further. Creating Color Contrast has been made easier with Color Hue Palettes. Designer's have taken the color wheel cut it up into certain elements and put these elements into usable color swatches. If you are not to sure what SWATCH means, it is the color palette that you choose your colors from, hence Color Swatch.

Back to Color Hue, which is basically the hue and saturation of a single color. Since we are provided an excellent color wheel already from Photoshop, we can use the Color Hue & Saturation Palette to create high contrast compositions.

Let's talk about three of these awesome color contrast schemes provided with Color Hue & Saturation, that you can use. ▶

MONOCHROMATIC COLOR HUE!

Monochromatic colors can be used to your advantage and can be very useful in the design process.

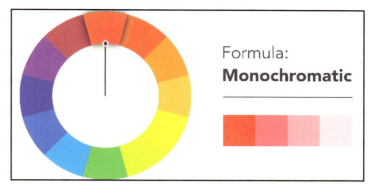

Formula:
Monochromatic

Monochromatic colors are all the colors that deal with a single color hue, which includes the tones, tints and shades of the color.

Basically created from overlapping colors from the color wheel, these are colors that are tint or shade variations of the same Color Hue. Lighter colors are often derived from this theory, unless of course you are dealing with colors with a darker temperature or color intensity.

Using this theory can be beneficial to you. Most people or the extreme think that color has to be chosen from the color wheel because these are your regular options of primary, secondary and tertiary color's. You know that choosing different color schemes and combinations can create equal vility between all elements used.

Color combinations can be tricky, but using the right shades and tones can drastically help keep maintain your ultimate goal, which is keeping a harmonious and visually cohesive design look and feel.

With the ability to use any color scheme, it's up to you to decide what colors to use. ▶

MONOCHROMATIC SHADES!

The one thing you do not want to happen is everything fading into a single background. This gives off a dense feel to a design, but also can cause your design to be stale with nothing standing out. Shades can enhance the ability of any element and make it appeal more, helping you add depth to your design.

When working with shades, you are taking the base color and adding black. With black being the darker color of the two your base color has the ability to stand out. Take this image of the flower to the right for example because it is a good image to showcase how shades can affect your image. By taking a rose and adding contrast shades to it, they are able to create depth that helps the rose stand out more.

You'll often use different versions of color shades to help contrast your type from each other and with this ability, you can create a more focused and an up-front focal point. Mixing color with the use of color shades can help even out your design and create a strong emphasis on certain elements in your design. ▶

MONOCHROMATIC TONES!

Using Monochromatic Tones will allow for a greater range of contrasting color tones that can be used to attract attention, create focus and add visual interest. With Tones you are able to add grey to pull back the intensity of a color. This has a huge benefit because it allows you to drain out the color that is overpowering your design.

You'll often run into colors that may be overpowering your design, with the excellent use of tones, you can fade and tone each color to how you see fit, increasing the appeal of your image.

PHOTOGRAPHERS OFTEN USE TONES!

You'll often see Monochromatic Tones in Photography because it can help add depth and intensity to model's, with the use of simple color balance. This is often thought of as using a lighting effect on images. ▶

MONOCHROMATIC TINTS!

Tints are exactly what they sound like. They help lighten the base color so it is seen as more visual and appealing. With Monochromatic Tints, you are able to take your base color and simply add white. Since your color scheme is based on variations of one color, you can use tones to blend and mix that color.

Mixing colors comes into play enormously in design, you will take this concept and use it on a daily basis. Focus on using the right tints to even out your color can come in handy becomes color combos can be so tricky to work with.

USING THE RIGHT SHADES, TONES & TINTS!

Make sure that if you do use these methods, that you are using them correctly. I say this because people tend to forget about what each method can do for their design and tend to go off one of the main primary color theories, instead of using shades, tones or tints, this could hinder you from creating balance.

Working with color's and mixing color's can become a little tricky if you are trying to combine darker color's. This is where tint's come in because with Tints they can help lighten a color and even out your color's so you can choose which color you think will be the primary color.

Working with tint's can be selective because you are basically adding white to a color, but if it's a dark color that you are not adding tint to, but other's do have it, you have to make sure that these elements don't cancel each other out. ▶

Balance is always the ultimate goal and using these method's can greatly help you in choosing the right color combo's to help create a sense of balance. Since its a delicate balance of finding the right shades, tones and tints to use, you can work with different color schemes to see if they match or they offset each other. Using these monochromatic method's can help you tremendously. ▶

Even though these colors come directly off of your color wheel, these color schemes use colors that are directly next to each other on the color wheel. Analogous color use stands out a little more from complimentary colors because instead of using the normal base of two colors, Analogous color's deal's with the ability to blend three colors together to create symmetry.

They are usually called Analogous because with these colors combined they usually create a sense of serenity and comfort. You'll see this colors used a lot in nature designs because they are more pleasing to the eye.

Since these colors match well with each other. you can use them in a variety of ways. You are not stuck to the old label of not having enough color, by being provided with three mix and match colors.

ANALOGOUS COLOR DOMINANCE!

Being that Analogous colors are groups of three colors next to each other on the color wheel, they do share a common color. Seeing that all three colors all share a common color, one color will remain your dominant color.

Most of the time this color tends to be a primary or secondary color, used to draw the attention of the viewer. You have to remember that color matters when it comes to appeal and finding the right color will matter even more in the long run.

Analogous colors often mimic the colors in our natural environment because they create a calm and relaxed feel to your design; this is why color matter's. You are not only trying to get two colors to mix and match, but you are adding a third color to add appeal and interest. Easier said then done, but if done right can be harmonious and pleasing to the eye. One thing I like about Analogous Colors is that the colors you choose can be any color's. ▶

CLASH OF COLORS!

The best thing with the Analogous Color Schemes is they are usually automatically harmonious and balanced. In other words, it's next to nearly impossible for the colors you choose to clash. As a result of these colors being so close together in the color wheel, it means they are almost all from the same relative family of colors.

Since these colors are generally from the same family, they will allow you the ability to mix and match different color schemes, without any clash between each of the color you choose to win. Remember with Analogous Color you are working with color's that are symmetrically next to each other on the color wheel, but also the blend's that the use of these color's create.

You can find the perfect blends to mix because you are creating these color's from the choice of your primary color's. Your Primary will most likely be the dominate color of the chosen color's, but you can find the right mixture to create the perfect color. ▶

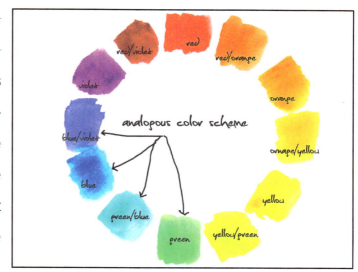

NATURALLY PLEASING!

Analogous Colors are meant to be pleasing, so use this to your advantage when you are looking at what colors to combine. It is often suggested that when choosing Analogous Color Schemes it is best to choose one primary or feature color and then choose two colors to take the supportive roles.

Since these colors can be naturally combined together, it makes everything a bit easier. Stay focused on using your colors to create pleasing designs. ▶

COMPLIMENTARY COLOR HUE

The last Color Scheme we will discuss is the Complimentary Color Hue. This is because Complimentary colors are the main colors that you will always use. These are your primary, secondary, and tertiary colors, sometimes referenced as Warm & Cool Color's and color schemes.

Since these colors are equally spaced on the color wheel, they are considered to be very exciting and dynamic colors. The principal of complementary color is defined by 3 color hues, primary, secondary and tertiary.

When ir comes to color, the base color you use will always be your primary color. Color is often based on the 3 primary colors which are always red, yellow and blue. Primary colors are the base for all color hues and any color can be created by using a combination of these primary colors.

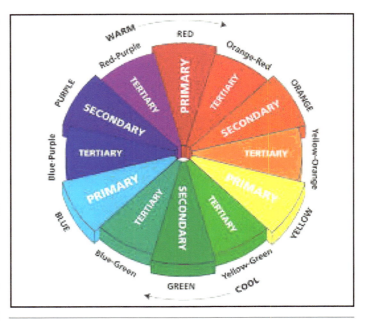

NUMEROUS COLOR CHOICES!

One thing about complimentary color's is that since the colors are often found adjacent to one another, it is easier to come up with color shades, tones and tints.

With a tremendous amount of color combination choices, you can always find the right colors to use. I like complimentary colors because using complementary color hues creates a high-drama, high-intensity and high-contrast look and feel to your design. One thing I hate is the stigma of Complimentary Colors. It is often said that you can't use Complimentary colors for larger designs because it offsets the design, and it's good to only use Complimentary Colors for small to medium size designs. I say WHY?

Focus on using the right schemes because it's up to you in the end. You can always find the right color combos to work with.

SPLIT COMPLIMENTARY COLORS!

Another version of Complimentary Color schemes you'll often here of is the Split-Complimentary color scheme. This color scheme can be used by taking your original color, a complimentary color and the two colors adjacent to your complimentary color.

In addition to the base color, it uses the two colors adjacent to its complementary color. This color scheme has the same strong visual contrast as the complementary color scheme, but has less tension. This follows the process of the three color's, but one color will definitely become your primary. ▶

DOUBLE COMPLIMENTARY COLORS!

Think of Complimentary Color Schemes with a twist, because that's what Double Complimentary color schemes are. A dual complementary scheme uses two colors side-by-side on the wheel and the pair of opposite colors created just from the left or right of the colors chosen. You are taking four colors to basically mix and match color's so you can create a primary base color.

Mixing colors comes into play enormously in design, but working with Double Complimentary Color schemes will only come into play sometimes. You are often mixing color's, but you will generally stick to the simple forms of Complimentary color's because these color's are often easier to work with. ▶

VALUE CONTRAST. When it comes to Contrast and even Color Schemes, Value can play a pivotal role in your design. Value Contrast is described as the lightness and darkness of your chosen color. Think of Value as how you see things, being that we use Value contrast in our everyday lives. We use Value to distinguish between light and dark, what's important what's not, what's emphasized to customers and clients and what's not. The ability to perceive things as we see them is what allows us to add Value to our perceptions.

VIEW YOUR WORLD!

Look around, take a moment to sit back and enjoy the scenery, so to speak. This is going to be what ultimately allows your inner creativity and ideas to come out. What you see, hear and feel on a daily basis, can be emphasized extremely in design. As we live in a three-dimensional world, you can create in a three-dimensional way. Since everyone perceives the world in a different way the ability to create and idealize new concepts and ideas can come just off looking

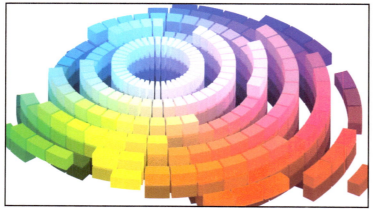

at other designer's and their work. Don't think of it as plagiarizing ideas, because you technically are not using that same exact concept. Since you are designing from a clear new perspective you can enhance what you know from other designers and add that knowledge to your designs.

Think of it as beneficial because Value helps you emphasize the focal point in your design, making it easier to distinguish what elements are more important then the other's. With this you create less confusion between you and the viewer or reader.

The ability to create the illusion of depth is a great asset of Value, since you can use gradations of different shades and tones to enhance your color's. Value is relative, meaning that no matter what color you use every element in your design will have Value to it. Your references of light and dark will play deeply into how your design turns out. ▶

Value Elements!

Color -- *You will use different elements in color contrast, because you are using the ability to blend between light and dark.*

View -- *A huge element that will come into play is the view you are trying to portray. Since you are designing with the different use of opposite elements, you can easily use Value to provide depth and intensity.*

Space -- *Luckily you have an abundance of space to work with, but remember, space can be your friend and enemy, so make sure you use space to your advantage.*

When there is less contrast between light and dark, edges and elements become difficult to perceive. Being that it is perceived that we are mostly reliant on our light to dark perception of objects rather than our color perception of those objects, this is where you can use Value Contrast as a huge tool.

COLOR HUE HAS VALUE!

When your working with color and color schemes you have to remember that color hue has value, the more light the higher the Value. The Value of the Contrast used is what gives us the ability to create that two or three dimensional design.

Take a painting for instance, the artist chooses what primary color to emphasize then adds depth and intensity to it by applying the addition of other secondary colors. The primary always takes presence in your design, but with the addition of other colors, you are able to create unique color concepts that you can easily apply. Your goal with size contrast is to create a sense of visual interest with your design.

Perception is everything and the way we perceive color is just part of that association. Since we live in color, color is always seen as the reflection of our daily lives. We see objects and elements and perceive their color, when in reality it's the reflection of that object that gives us that color. I seen an awesome helicopter example on the weather channel.

In the desert U.S. Military helicopters would take off in the night and in the process their wings would showcase these awesome glowing halo's. The sand gives off the reflection of light and therefore you are seeing that light being casted upon the helicopters wings as the sand is kicked from the spin creating cool glowing halo's. ▶

THE VALUES OF SPACE!

Using Value allows you to create space between your elements. We have to perpetuate the single notion that space can be your friend, but to much a bad friend. The lighter a shape against a dark background, the more separation is perceived, and the same as if it was darker shapes against lighter backgrounds.

By emphasizing Value in certain elements of a design, you can create visual interest and areas of focus. Since Value is to be perceived through Contrast, this gives you the ability to define emphasis.

You are always going to be looking to keep a solid balance of space when it comes to design. What the goal is, is to use Value to differentiate the space you have between elements, because this is what ultimately creates the illusion of the design. The viewer will get a better understanding by simply looking at the color of the element and predicts where it leads. ▶

THE VALUES OF SPACE!

Using Value allows you to create space between your elements. We have to perpetuate the single notion that space can be your friend, but to much a bad friend. The lighter a shape against a dark background, the more separation is perceived, and the same as if it was darker shapes against lighter backgrounds.

By emphasizing Value in certain elements of a design, you can create visual interest and areas of focus. Since Value is to be perceived through Contrast, this gives you the ability to define emphasis. ▶

THE DEGREE OF LIGHT & DARK!

Since light and dark are opposites, using Value with contrast can bring your objects forward, but also organize the rest of the elements to keep symmetrical balance, suggesting an illusion of space in a two-dimensional design.

Focus on what degree you want to apply with your Values. Picking the right color shades, tones and tints can easily help establish your concept of colors. Remember with Value Contrast your using lightness and darkness of colors to define forms and create visual illusions of interest. ▶

THE DEGREE OF LIGHT & DARK!

Since light and dark are opposites, using Value with contrast can bring your objects forward, but also organize the rest of the elements to keep symmetrical balance, suggesting an illusion of space in a two-dimensional design.

Focus on what degree you want to apply with your Values. Picking the right color shades, tones and tints can easily help establish your concept of colors. Remember with Value Contrast your using lightness and darkness of colors to define forms and create visual illusions of interest. ▶

TYPE CONTRAST. The last method we will discuss is Type Contrast. Type contrast is exactly what it sounds like it is, all about typography. Creating a clear focal point in your designs can be pretty difficult if you're trying to make things as similar or symmetrical as possible to keep balance. For example, Type with the same size, color and weight will likely end up being boring and uninteresting. With Type Contrast you can change all that with the simple ease of direction. Making more important bigger fonts stand out then other smaller fonts can give direction to the reader or viewer. .

THE USE OF TYPOGRAPHY!

When you use more than one font or type in your designs to achieve contrast, you'll need to make sure the font pairings go well together and are visually distinct from one another. The fonts need to be able to create separation and in doing this it allows the readers to not get confused trying to figure out the message. Your ability is also not limited here. with the use of typography you are able to use different font weight and styles to complete the job. One thing about fonts is that their is a new Font created daily. Designer's all over the world are developing new fonts as we speak. This enhances our abilities greatly because most if not half of these fonts are free to download and use. Please note though, when it comes to font's if it has a license make sure you have the designer's permission to use it.

There has been quite a bit of designer's who got screwed using font's when they didn't know that the font they used was copyrighted. Please also note that don't let that scare you away because there are still plenty of fonts out there that are downloadable and free to use. Also there are awesome tool's to use such as; Fontjoy and Type Connection, which are web sites that come up with font pairs for you.

Using different font styles, color and weights can also be a great plus because these three elements gives you the ability to use several font pairs in your designs. ▶

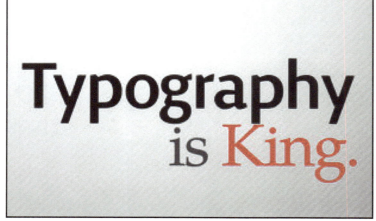

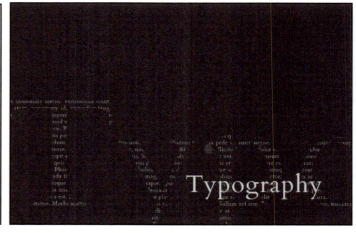

THE RIGHT STYLE SAYS IT ALL!

The style of font you use can make a huge difference in the way your design is displayed or interpreted. The benefit is that there are numerous font styles to choose from, whether you are looking for a simple elegant font or a more intrusive font. Font styles can play a big role in cementing the overall look of your design, especially if you're trying to create visual interest.

Keep in mind your choice of font and how it works with your layout, grid, color scheme will make the difference between a good, bad and great design. You are working with two types of elements here. Your working with fonts but your also working with the typefaces of those fonts. What I mean by this is that Fonts are a group of typefaces that have the same or similar characteristics, while typefaces refer to the family member of that font. Typography places a major role in your design because in typography, contrast refers to weight contrast, which is to say that contrast denotes the difference between thick and thin typefaces. The greater the weight, the greater the contrast can be, while the lower the weight, the lower the contrast. ▶

MAKE SOME of the words more **IMPORTANT** by varying their **SIZE**

TYPOGRAPHY & HIERARCHY!

We have talked about hierarchy when it comes to contrast and typography is no different. Typography is used to create depth and emphasis within your design so you can create focus. Your ultimate goal is to reinforce your text and your message, if done wrong typography can be unpleasant and boring. Web designers use this thinking all the time because we see a hierarchy in the pages and layouts we design.

Using Typography Contrast is important because not all the content within a design has the same value, some elements have greater significance or hierarchy than other elements. By creating contrast, you can direct the reader's attention to the important messages but also at the same time enhance the visual appearance and interest. ▶

TYPOGRAPHIC SIZE IN CONTRAST!

The most common use of Typographic Contrast is Size. This is because it is the one main common method used to create distinction between common elements. The concept is fairly simple, you take your larger more important type and apply them in a way where it keeps the smaller type legible and readable.

You want functionality in your design and by contrasting large type with small type we get a visually appealing typographical design with functionality. One thing with type is that you never want to use the exact same size or font for your design, doing this creates a bland design with no interest or appeal.

You want to use variety, but at the same time keep your type size in sync with your design. Take a look at these images for example. Most quotes can often be seen as examples because they show how the different font size use helps there focal point stand out, adding appeal to the design. ▶

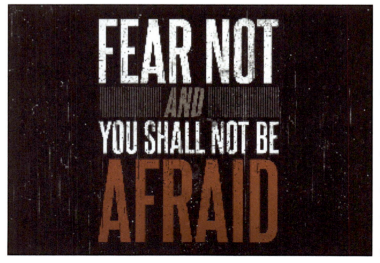

TYPOGRAPHIC SHAPE IN CONTRAST!

Now I know your thinking what does shapes have to do with Typography, well I am not talking about shapes indirectly, what I am referring to is the shape of using different typefaces or weight to alter your type. Shape probably has the most capability to create contrast because it depends on the use of several typefaces.

Be careful because it is easy to design elements that really detract from everything else in the design because they simply command too much attention. For example, to many fonts in one design can cause each font to try and vy for attention, and in turn can cause confusion and disarray. So focus on using the right balance with type shapes. ▶

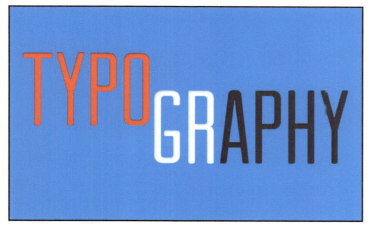

TYPOGRAPHIC COLOR IN CONTRAST!

The second most common Typographic Contrast method is Color Typography, which in itself is a great benefit. The most common way that we see this in design is having some type color lighter than others. Obviously lighter text has less strength and creates less visual attention, causing a contrast between any darker element.

Color also helps establish a visual hierarchy because the most important elements will command the most visual attention, while the other colors or type play the supportive role. Hierarchy is important in Color because, your elements will always compete with each other. The hierarchy or structure is what provides you that sense of balance. As we discussed numerous times, Balance plays a tremendous role in the design process because it affects a number of elements.

Balance is created by the use of color's, typography, contrast, size, shape, texture's, color's of type, color's of images, color blending with images, color contrast, size contrast, value contrast, and a number of other options, so it plays a vital role.

Back to Color Typography in Contrast. Since Color already play's a pivotal role in your design process, using the right color's with font's can help you create emphasis on your focal point. Using bigger and darker color's will obviously increase the chance of visual interpretation, rather then seeing smaller lighter type that has no visual appeal.

Visual appeal is what Type Color Contrast is all about because Color itself is such a character driven emotional tool that we use in our everyday lives. ▶

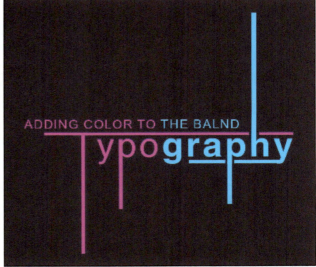

TYPE. I wanna talk a little more about Type. Since typography is one of the main things in design, I wanna discuss typography and typefaces a little more. Since typography is what ultimately creates hierarchy and emphasis it is one of the main methods that is always used in design. The basis of typography ranges and you will always be learning about new typefaces and fonts.

THE WEIGHT OF THE WORLD

Ok maybe not the world but I want you to think about this analogy because I want you to think big. Thicker may not always be better but in design emphasis; it is. It helps you display key information that can be easily perceived. Since typefaces come in many weights, it's up to you to use them the way you want to. When it comes to the weight of a font you are choosing the thickness of the character outline relative to the font's height. The one good thing is that weight can be easily distributed and can help put focus on your type or angle you are trying to supply.

You'll often see many weight variations in a single font. These typefaces are available for you to choose from, but the most common are semi-bold, bold and black. Used primarily to achieve emphasis and impact, these awesome typefaces are usually available for each font type. Keep in mind that some custom created and designed font's might not have them.

ADDING STYLE TO THE BLAND!

It is funny how something that is so simple can make such a huge difference. We are talking about the Italic & Oblique Styles. Many font families have an italics version of the font. The italic font style of a typeface has been slanted to the right and has had other minor changes made to the letter glyphs to make them slightly different.

With this slight difference the font becomes more of a handwritten, cursive styled font. This is often used with Script font's. Since typical Script font's are sometimes naturally curved and slanted they give you a good mixture of elegance and harmony. You might not think of it but there are font's out there that are designed to look exactly like it's been handwritten or made to look like it was strictly written in cursive.

The other awesome style we typically use is the Oblique Style, which is totally different then the Italic Style. The Oblique Style characters are also slanted but, unlike italics, the glyphs themselves are not changed or edited. Oblique styled fonts are not related to italics because they lack the change in letter shapes which is part of the definition of "Italic". ▶

How to pair fonts? Don't use too similar.

A SERIF IN THE FAMILY!

You will use a lot of styles in your design but with Font the most common style that of course is used is the easy addition of Sans-Serif and Serif fonts. One thing that easily easily seen is that these two types of font's are easily distinguishable. One thing you will often see is that Serif font's are some of the oldest modern typefaces.

You'll notice Serif typefaces by identifying the letters in your font with small feet or lines on the ends of the letter's associated with the font. Serif Typefaces are generally thought to give the look of a more serious or traditional design. Remember that typeface is the design and the font is how that design is displayed or delivered.

Although serifs are considered to be decorative, their appearance may well serve a higher purpose. Serif typefaces have been credited with increasing both the readability and visual interest of your design. Since these typefaces tend to change daily, whether they are made better or newly created, studying them can really enhance your capabilities and abilities.

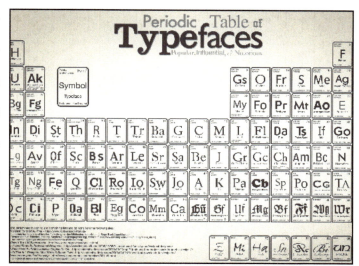

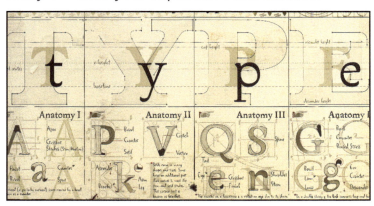

Gather a few font examples to use when it comes to Serif typefaces because although you will ultimately use Sans and Serif font's the mixture of the two can be made more smooth and easily legible.

SANS & SANS-SERIF!

Traditional, modern and often most used is of course is your Sans and Sans-Serif Typefaces. Sans and Sans-Serif Font's are the most common and modern font's that are used in design. As simple as they sound, these font's are font typefaces that don't have the extra little accents that Serif's have, but they give you that more modern and traditional look and feel.

Think of readability and what it looks like to the reader, because it's ultimately up to them if your information gets processed. Sans and Sans-Serif typefaces usually don't have that decorative look as Serif's do, but you will be able to use it as a more pleasant and readable font choice. ▶

Ultralight
Thin
Light
Regular
Medium
Semibold
Bold
Heavy
Black

**TYPOGRAPHY
MATTERS**

Remember that this is one of your best contrast forms to use. Since we often are trying to apply emphasis on our design's, using type contrast can easily help you accomplish this. You are provided with a variety of different forms or methods of type contrast to use and each element has it's own advantages.

Using these advantages gives you one up on other designer's because you are using your full capabilities of design, not limiting yourself to the simple standard. Concentrate on using the right weight's to help add contrast, using the right color's and sized font's, but also don't forget about placement when you are working with Typography and Type Contrast.

Placing you elements so they contrast each other, can help you figure out the hierarchy of the information you are providing. Understanding the hierarchy of your typography allows you to better comprehend how your design will come out and howyour design will be seen by your viewer. ▶

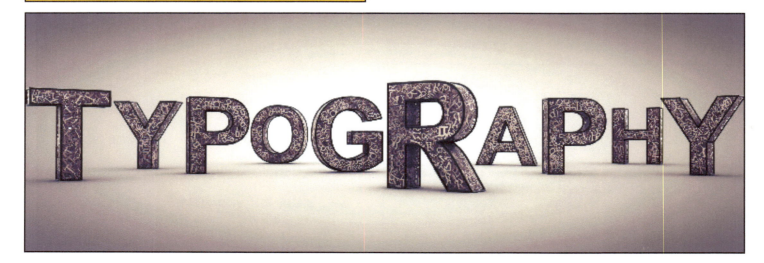

LEARN FROM QUOTES!

If you ever need a little hint of an idea too how placement or type contrast can ultimately work for you, check out examples of Quotes. These are the perfect examples of contrast because they are displayed it a way to draw in the viewer's eyes to the focal point, then gives direction from there. This is very important because without the right focal point to concentrate or focus on, your viewer can get lost in your design.

You can also use these examples for examples of how weight and size type contrast is used, because designer's will often showcase different sized type with different weight's to create contrast in their designs. Quotes are popular for lot's of reason's, but gather ideas off the them because they will help you. ▶

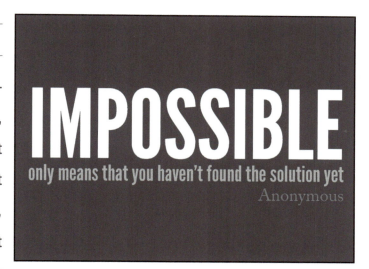

REMEMBER THESE QUICK CONTRAST LEARNING TIPS!

1 SIZE - size plays an important role in Contrast. You are often referring to this when you place your elements on your page. The main key to contrast is making sure there is an obvious difference. Think of quotes when you are thinking about size, because they can help.

2 COLOR - color can be your enemy, but if utilized right can be your best friend. Color play's a powerful role in your design and it's how you utilize this power that's left up to you. Color is utilized greatly in design because it is the one element that is a constant in the design process.

3 VALUE - when it comes to using the right color scheme, Value can play a pivotal role. Value Contrast is described as the lightness and darkness if your color. Adding Value can tremendously even out your design, but help draw out your main elements and create emphasis for them.

4 TYPE - the aim of your typography will play a pivotal role in finding what's useful and what's not. You will also want to use this to your advantage because really dull, boring and unpleasant design's can easily be made pleasing with the simple use of typography and Type Contrast.

BALANCE. In learning the design process, you will learn a tremendous amount about Balance and what exactly it entails. As in life, having balance allows you to live a healthy stable life, such is needed in design. Using Balance can give you that extra visual interpretation, seeing that Balance adds depth and density to any design. You always want to find the right Balance in your design, because this is one of the concepts that you can really use to your advantage and draw in that attention.

THE BALANCE OF DESIGN!

Balance in design is the distribution of your used elements in the design, but also the distribution of the visual weight of objects, fonts, colors, textures, and shapes. You want to place your elements in a way that the Balance of your design gives of a visual interpretation, seeing that large, denser elements or objects appear to be heavier while smaller elements or objects appear to be lighter. Your placement of these elements or objects is what comes into play.

Since you want to keep your elements placed in a symmetrical balance, you often use Balance to display how the page will look. What I love about Balance is that you can easily use it to draw in your readers attention and to easily create a focal point.

Use Balance to add stability, structure, create emphasis, interpretation and create dynamics in your design. In design, your goal is to place your visual elements in an aesthetically pleasing arrangement that is balanced, but still has a certain look and feel.

Think of it Placement as key commodity, too much can offset your design, to little can throw off your balance, so you have to find the right balance in your design. When it comes to Balance you will only really deal with Three Main Methods of Balance. These are Symmetrical Balance, Asymmetrical Balance and Radial Balance, these will also be the main methods we'll be learning about. All three of these have beneficial use, some more then others. ▶

SYMMETRY BALANCE IN DESIGN!

The most common type and formal use of Balance is working with Symmetry. Symmetrical balance can be used to achieve a formal design, a sense of structure, and also have a sense of organization and stability. The ultimate goal is to create and arrange your elements in a way that they are equally balanced on either side of your central axis.

Think of it as drawing a straight line down the center of the page, all the visual elements on one side of the page are mirrored on the other side, creating equal balance in your design. When you are designing your central axis or central starting line it can be vertical

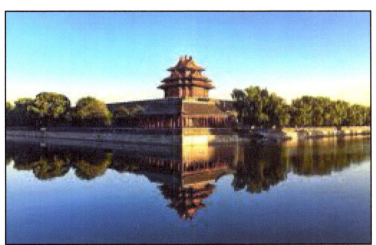

or horizontal. This decision is mostly all dependant on you and the way you choose to design. Since symmetrical balance can be accomplished by using ether method, it ultimately comes down to you. Symmetrical balance can be thought of as 50/50 balance or like a mirror image. In other words, the elements would look the same on either side of the center axis.

You view this in everyday life. Ever look in a mirror? The image that is placed back to you is totally symmetrical to you, because it's the exact image of you.

This is what keeping symmetrical balance is all about, you want your design to maintain a constant look of appeal, while keeping balance and harmony. Without either your design lacks that visual interpretation and fails, becoming very unpleasant and boring to your reader's.

The structure and consistency of your design is very important and since Symmetrical Balance can keep every element aligned the way you want it, you can use it to provide order, clarity and solid consistency. Keeping balance makes it easy for our eyes to follow shapes and patterns that are repeated in sequence.

Focus on using the right balance to keep your visual appeal and interest, it's easier for your reader to attain your design. ▶

When it comes to Symmetrical Balance you are basing your design of a center point or center axis. With the ability to create perpetual balance off an either horizontal or vertical axis, you can make sure your elements are easily mirrored like one another.

With this ability you can keep your elements equally distributed on both sides of your design, whether you are designing off of either a horizontal or vertical center point or central axis. However you choose to start your design you can easily see with the images below that; either way, each one can be beneficial.

Most landscape and scenery design's will often resemble the ambiance of Horizontal Symmetrical Balance. They use this form because as you can see with the image directly below, it's easy to create a symmetrical balance with even placement of your elements. In this image the elements are a beautiful palace just split down the horizontal line.

With Photoshop you are able to mix and blend images together with the simple use of tools and layers. With this you are able to create amazing design's, that gives off the look of an even and Symmetrically Balanced design and image. ▶

Balance Elements In The Design Process!

Symmetrical -- *The most formal use of Balance, Symmetrical Balance is more focused on the use of a line down the center of a page.*

Asymmetrical -- *Not based of a straight line, with Asymmetrical Balance you take a more unbalanced approach not focusing on symmetry.*

Radial -- *Kinda what it sounds like, Radial Balance is the use of balance with elements that radiate out from a center point in a circular fashion.*

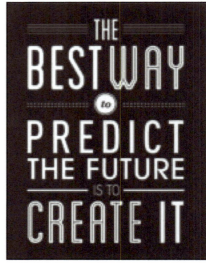

THE BEST WAY to PREDICT THE FUTURE IS TO CREATE IT

EQUAL DISTRIBUTION IN BALANCE!

Placement of element's with equality means that you will be working with different images to make them blend in a way that they create equal distribution within your design. If you are not to sure what I mean by this, take a look at the picture above. I chose this image because it replicates the use of equal weighted distribution between the same image. The image gives off a sense of balance, and in all reality, it's really just the same image, flipped vertical and blended to give off that reflection look and feel.

This is what equal distribution is all about. Using equality between two images or elements to create a unique symmetrical balance. Since each element is of the same manner, you can easily place them in a way that your viewer easily understand's the concept of the design. Just as the above image is a great example of Horizontal Distribution, the design to the right is another prime example of equal distribution, but it is a little different. This design is based off of a Vertical Axis, but also help's keep the two element's in sync and symmetrical with each other.

Equal distribution can be key to a good symmetrical balanced design. Since weight plays a major role in contrast it can be the same here. Think of it as using a balancing scale, if you have to much you easily lose balance and of course to little the same outcome.

You have to use the right equal amounts of distribution because this can be what offsets your design. You are designing off an axis and you want your elements to coincide with each other. When elements coincide with each other, it's easier to mirror and arrange your elements so the design flows and has perfect symmetry. ▶

EQUAL WEIGHT WITH YOUR ELEMENTS!

Symmetrical balance is the one of the main principal's of design because of the role it plays. Since Symmetrical Balanced designs often give off a look of formality, it is one of the most typically used methods of Balance.

We've talked about weight before and that's exactly what symmetrical designs are all about. Symmetrical Balance refers to the balance that is achieved by arranging elements on either side of the center of a composition in an equally weighted manner.

Symmetry is when elements are arranged in the same way on both sides of the center point of your axis. This takes place when elements are mirrored over the axis and exactly the same on both sides.

With Symmetry comes Balance which is simply the concept of visual equality, and relates to the perception we have when it comes to sense of balance. Different elements of weight is what gives off this perception or visual equality because they are arranged in a way that is aesthetically pleasing and enjoyable to the viewer.

Since balance is a huge concept of Symmetry your aim is to create a focal point that helps you emphasize your design, allowing your viewer to see the whole picture. Equally weighted elements or objects can also help you achieve direction because they are displayed in an Equally Weighted Manner. Direction goes right along with Perception because how we perceive things is what gives us the direction to go. With Symmetrical Balance you are doing just that, you are giving your viewer something to perceive, and then take direction from their.

Perception plays a key role in Balance because once something is easily perceived, it tends to be easier to understand. I say this because your goal is creating a design that is easily perceived, if the viewer is thrown off by your design, it can be more complicated to understand and may be less legible then you think. ▶

DEPTH OF PERCEPTION!

Direction in design can sometimes be described as the way one perceives the way the design is supposed to be read. In reality Direction is described as the course or path the eye is perceived to go. For designers this is sometimes hard to tell, that is why most articles and posts you see today will describe several ways of Direction use.

One thing you can always count on is that when your design is symmetrically balanced your designs stay proportional. Adding depth and density to your design allows you to create a better emphasis within your design. Color is a great way to object perception because with color it allows your eyes to be drawn to a certain element in your composition.

Since the colors you use will effect your design's perception drastically, it's all about finding the right balance between colors and colors schemes. As our eyes perceive thing's as we see them, we are drawn to color's that appeal to us or add visual intrigue.

Perception is often the key to graphic design because what we see and perceive can be extruded in so many ways. Not everyone has the ability to see color as we do, so keep in mind that you are designing to create emphasis, but if the color's can't be seen, you have to make sure you create that emphasis through perception, allowing the viewer to easily follow the flow of the design. Creating with the depth of perception also gives you the ability to see how the design will lay out and how the element's will blend with each other when the design is completed. ▶

DYNAMIC PANORAMA IMAGES!

One great thing with Symmetrical Balance is the ability to give of these amazing panorama views. These awesome designs give you a sense of harmony and serenity. Since they often give off a sense of relaxation, these awesome designs can be enjoyed by everyone. ▶

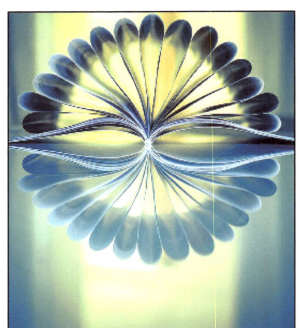

LIGHT TO DARK CONTRAST!

As previously discussed, we use the transition for light to dark in a lot of symmetrical designs. With this you are able to create depth and intensity to help bring out certain colors and visual interest's. Whether you are designing in a radial symmetrical form or the normal symmetrical form, you can accomplish anything you set your mind to, keeping your designs balanced and harmonious. ▶

ENJOYABLE CLASSIC ARTWORKS!

Symmetrical Balance has always played a valuable role in some classic art pictures. Since this is such a valuable asset, you will tend to see it in a lot of classical artwork designs or custom artwork pieces. ▶

SYMMETRY IN ARCHITECTURE!

One of the most common places you will find the use if symmetrical balance is in Architecture. Architect's will often use this method because it allows them to provide a stable, steady and reliable foundation to work with.

Although it is probably easier then other design methods, it clearly provides you the contrast between balanced elements. Architecture is always the expression of the architect tself, so it kinda mimic's the principle of Color here. Since color gives of expression, same thing can be said for architecture. Architecture, whether it is art on a wall or built in a standard form uses the concept's of all balance theories, whether it be symmetrical, asymmetrical or radial.

NOTHING ON EARTH
COULD COME BETWEEN THEM

One of the best examples of Symmetrical Balance is this Titanic poster because of the way the actor's and ship is layed out. The ship is used to cause a symmetrical look to create the contrast of both elements being the same. ▶

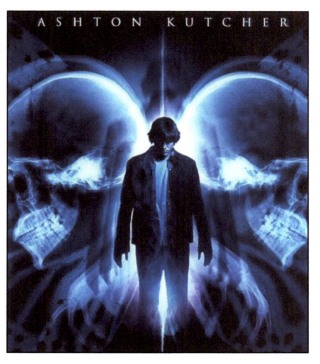

ASHTON KUTCHER

THE MOVIES WE LOVE!

Take some of your classic and favorite movies and their posters. The Poster's are design in an aesthetically pleasing way that it provides intrigue for the viewer, as they ultimately go to see the film.

These Movie Poster's are used to draw in the viewers attention, but keep a sense of balance so it does not over due the concept. They use a symmetrical balance perfectly with the blend of characters and color. This is often seen and used to help distinguish character's and actor's. ▶

ASYMMETRICAL BALANCE IN DESIGN!

Unbalanced is the key here, and with this ability you are not restricted to the symmetrical side of balance. With Asymmetrical Balance you are taking a different approach to your design. The use of Asymmetrical Balance takes a different step towards design with an unbalanced look and feel. You are still working with opposite elements, but these elements are not identical to one another and they differ from each other in every way.

The key is to still place these elements and arrange these elements in a way that there is still a sense of Balance. The pure definition of asymmetry is of course objects and elements that lack symmetry, but keep a sense of harmony and balance.

When using Asymmetrical Balance in design you are not limited to the adaptation of having your elements exactly the same to create that sense of balance, but a rather unorthodox way of placing elements in an unparalleled design that doesn't have equal distribution in the composition.

Whenever we create a design that consists of elements that we've distributed unevenly you'll have an asymmetrical design. You can use it to draw attention to areas in the design or to convey dynamism or movement.

The flow of your design can be beneficial with an Asymmetrical Balance, since it's seen as more off-setting. For example, a large area full of dull color can be balanced out by a much smaller area of brighter color.

Same goes for shapes and objects, a small very complex shape can be balanced by a larger simpler shape. With Asymmetrical Balance your elements on either side of a composition do not reflect one another, therefore it can be hard to keep a sense of balance, but when done well it can result in beautiful and eye-catching designs.

Since you are using different elements to provide and keep a sense of balance, focus on the right elements to blend. ▶

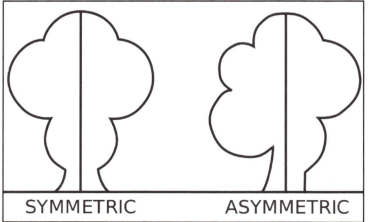

SYMMETRIC   ASYMMETRIC

ORGANIZATION TO CHAOS!

One thing you will always hear with using Asymmetrical Balance is that your bringing organization to chaos. The elements you are using are off-balanced and offset, but you still have the ability to bring organization to chaos. Off-balanced elements have the ability to add a different feel to your design, creating a different aspect of intrigument.

In most online polls viewer's have said that Asymmetrical Balanced designs are more visually interesting and dynamic. Since you are not stuck to the norm with Asymmetrical Balance, your design has more depth, appeal and visual interest.

The goal is to draw in your reader's attention with just a few images, this can sometimes be hard to do, but with the right balance you can achieve these goals.

Asymmetrical design is essential when you are trying to draw in the audience. Not only does it bring order to chaos, but it helps you develop in an unbalanced manner. Although designing on an unbalanced platform can be a bit tricky, the resulting outcome of the design is well worth it.

Your goal is to bring order to chaos, which is always easier said then done, but when done right can mean a whole world of difference. Use your creative thinking and you'll come up with ideas for ways to keep order.

Chaos keeps the world evolving in my mind, because there is so much chaos going on in the world, it's hard to keep track of what's going on. Not with Asymmetrical Balance, though the concept's may seem the same with Asymmetrical Balance you are able to bring some kind of organization to this unorthodox way of chaos. ▶

DIFFERENT ELEMENTS IN USE!

Using different sizes, shapes and colors is one of the fun things about design. You will often recognize Asymmetrical designs in a lot of print and media you see today. They use different elements to project their message and information. This message is often described with the use of different elements placed and arranged in a way that the viewer's eyes are instantly attracted to a certain word or color.

This is where the use of different sizes, shapes and colors comes into play. The easiest example to use, is the example of a puzzle. When you look at a puzzle, you are looking at tons of pieces that have color and design to them, but when placed all together they create a unique image. This is because even though these puzzle pieces are all different in their own right, they are created in a way to keep the puzzle balanced when it is all put together. You can think of the design process of Asymmetrical Balance the same way.

You are using non-identical elements to create a sense of placement and interest. If your viewer technically read's from left to right, you have the ability to focus on stronger elements on the left, while the elements on the right help keep everything aligned and balanced.

You'll see the terms of nonidentical, or unsymmetrical, and this simply refers to elements that are not exactly the same or are not in exact symmetry with each other. Therefore the use of different sizes, shapes and color's can be a huge benefit because it gives you the ability to add this depth and imbalance to your design. Detail is in the eye of the beholder, and creating eye-catching material is the way to go.

You are never limited with the uses of different methods. With the ability to add different sizes, shapes and color, you are easily able to create a focal point in your design or create emphasis on certain elements to help them stand out more. Use this method when you are working with typography also because with different sized typography you can easily create drastic appeal. ▶

OPPOSITES & COLORS CAN ATTRACT!

Unbalanced and totally opposite elements are the key to good visual representation and balance. As we have discussed before, you are taking opposite elements and placing them in a way that gives off balance and visual interest.

When it comes to choosing opposite elements think of it as elements placed with weight and direction. I say this because within a certain composition the weight of your elements is what draws in the attention of the viewer's eyes. With direction your designing in a way described as the course the viewer's eyes are perceived to take. With these two element methods you can think of how to place your images

and elements to help create visual contrast that keeps a sense of balance. For example, darker colors are placed with lighter colors to offset image placement, drawing in your viewer.

You will also see larger portions of color offset by smaller portions of color. One thing about opposite colors is that they can easily be manipulated, because there are so many choices for color and color contrast, you have multiple options to choose from. Asymmetrical Balance is a delicate balance of offset images, so make sure when you place your element's your looking at every concept possible.

Don't limit yourself when you are using Asymmetrical Design because this is ultimately where your creative mind can come into play. Remember that opposites can attract and finding the right opposite elements to use and blend can turn into some amazing design's. Use color to add different contrast's within your design to make sure these opposites do attract, creating an easy design flow. ▶

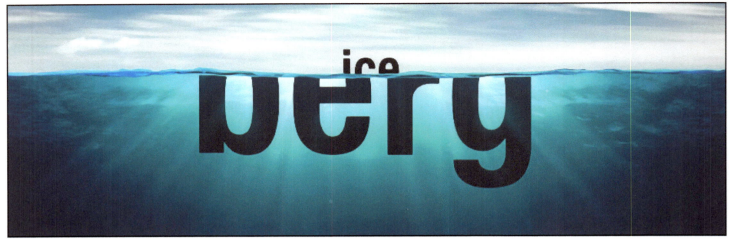

USING THE RIGHT TYPOGRAPHY!

Check out this awesome use of Asymmetrical Balance. This custom design was designed with the use of excellent font difference and choices. With a different blend and take on balance, they were able to create emphasis and visual appeal. ▶

ASYMMETRY IN PHOTOGRAPHY!

Asymmetrical designs are often used in photography because it provides a better understanding of depth. You can easily use it to project your image in an unbalanced manner, but the image stays balanced. ▶

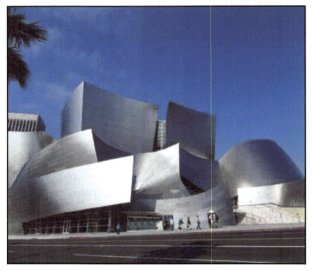

WE ALL LOVE QUOTES!

Nothing makes us happier then seeing cool quotes. Asymmetrical Balance allows you to add visual depth and appeal to your quotes.

With the addition of backgrounds and colors, these quotes can be turned into cool themed designs. With the ability of different font use and weight, we are able to add contrast and visual appeal. ▶

RADIAL SYMMETRY IN DESIGN!

The last form of balance we will discuss is Radial Symmetry in Balance. Which in all reality is almost identical to symmetrical balance, but does have a few different advantages to it.

Radial Balance involves your elements situated equally around the center point of your design. Think of something like a clock, there is a central point where the clock hands meet, the hands turning from this central point, and an equal number of digits on either side of the center point.

Your goal is to create a symmetrical balanced design of a single center point that you choose. One thing about Radial Symmetry is that your center point, does not have to be the center point of the page. Your center point can be chosen from any side or section of your design. With the ability to create radial symmetry with the whole page, you have an abundance of options to start with.

Focus on using the right radial symmetrical balance to keep your visual appeal and interest, because the depth of perception will play a huge role in Radial Symmetry, so use this form of balance wisely.

RADIAL SYMMETRY BALANCE!

If you remember Math, you'll remember that a radius is based off of the distance between the center of a circle on your page and it's edge. This concept helps explain what radial symmetry is, visual elements arranged around a center point, taking a circular form to symmetry.

Radial keeps of form of symmetry by using elements situated in an equally weighted manner around this center point. This allows you to keep a symmetrical balance to your design, creating a visual interest to draw in your viewer. ▶

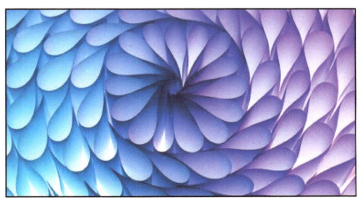

CENTER POINT OF INTEREST!

As we previously discussed the center of attraction is everything in design. I say this because when it comes to design there are so many assets that can go into one simple decision. Think of it this way, when you are designing you have to take into consideration the visual depth, interest, appeal, readability, legibility, contrast between elements, contrast between colors , balance of elements and more.

You are taking the elements and arranging them in an aesthetically pleasing way, so it is easier if you focus and base your design off of one central focul

point. Not only does this make designing and creating more simpler, but it allows you to think in all forms of Balance. Since you will be using the arrangement of types, color 's and shapes, you can easily keep your elements balanced in a pleasant manner.

Readability and legibility are key rules to design, because they are what can attract your reader's attention easier. You use these Center Focul Points to make it easier to understand, but also add visual depth. Since no design is ever the same, you have the ability to create visually interesting artwork that appeals to your viewers. There are several ways to provide Symmetry in your design and because of this a lot of designs will often have some form of Radial Balance.

In design, there is always going to be a clear center point, and the individual elements of the design will radiate outward equally from it. You can use this to focus on using the right form of Radial Balance to keep your design visually appealing and interesting, allowing your reader to attain your design. Since this is what we are trying to accomplish, use this form accordingly. ▶

CENTER OF ATTRACTION!

Like in Symmetrical Balance you are basing your design of a center point or central axis, but with Radial it is not a straight line. With Radial Balance you are creating a visual perception of both Symmetrical and Asymmetrical Balance. Take the image to the right for example. The design is based of a central point and is created to give off off the illusion of Balance, but it a radial form.

This is because even though the design might look offset, it is actually balanced of from the center point. Using the right elements can draw in your viewer with the use of good balance.

With Radial Symmetry it's easier to create a sense of balance by simply applying the right contrast between your elements. You want elements to coincide with each other, but not look unbalanced. Doing this can create a sense of depth to your design al owing the viewer to understand the concept. This illusion is given off by our visual perception of depth. Since you know automatically that the design references a clock, once you look at the design, you perceive the direction the design is supposed to go.

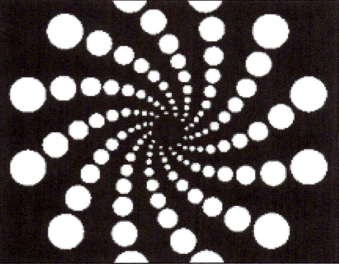

You are designing from the moment you choose your center point. Once this center point is designated, it is then easier for you to focus on using and blending the right elements together to create that visual depth, all the while using the foundation of a circular form of balance. ▶

COLOR. In learning the basics, the last principal we will talk about is of course COLOR. Color plays the ultimate role in your design because it's what ultimately draw's in your viewer's attention. With color you have the ability to add depth and intensity to certain elements to help draw them out from the rest of your concept. This can add the illusion of appeal because it draw's in the viewer's eyes to certain elements arranged to create emphasis on these elements.

THE BALANCE OF COLOR!

Balance in design is the distribution of your elements in the design placed in an aesthetically pleasing way, but is also the distribution of the visual weight of color that enhances these elements to create that balance.

Perception is key and Color is the key to perception because what we see is what we perceive. This perception ultimately gives us the direction our eyes follow, or the flow of the design.

Since what we see first is said to be what we instantly perceive, the Color you first recognize is usually what creates your Focul Point. If the emphasized element is instantly perceived it usually come's across easier for your viewer's to read or understand.

Color is amazing because it can create appeal and interest by combining the use of multiple color schemes. As we discussed before in Color Contrast, finding the right color combination in color schemes can easily add visual interest and depth to your design. ▶

Color Elements!

Warm Color's -- *These are the lighter colors such as fire, fall leaves, and sunsets and sunrises, and are generally thought of as energizing, passionate, and positive.*

Cool Color's -- *These colors are usually of night, water, nature, and are usually described as calming, relaxing, and somewhat reserved.*

Color Schemes -- *The mixture of multiple color's and color hues that are used to create emphasis and appeal.*

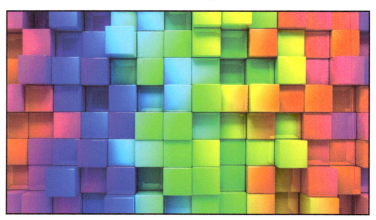

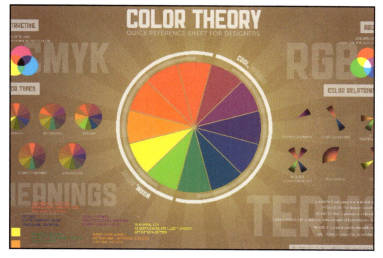

The Color Wheel was created to help you learn the difference between tones, shades and tints, while developing color schemes. Since Color itself, is ever-changing, the Color Wheel helps you develop color schemes and combinations that wont easily cancel each other out. Color itself can be tricky to work with, sometimes blending two colors you like might not necessarily blend together. It is your job to find out what colors you can use to match and what color's that wont go together. In a sense your finding the Balance between color's that can easily be worked with.

Study the Color Wheel as it will often help you decide on what color's to choose and what color's to stay away from. Since Color is a mixture of different elements, it too can be easily manipulated but also often overdone. Your goal is for a sense of balance, without adding to much color. ▶

THE ALL MIGHTY COLOR WHEEL!

Here is where it all begins with color. Your Color Wheel is the main attribute that you will be using to create your color schemes. Color is an enriched element and not knowing where to start can lead you down the wrong path.

Knowing about color concepts, hues and color schemes allows you to create specific pairs of color's that you can easily use and manipulate within your designs.

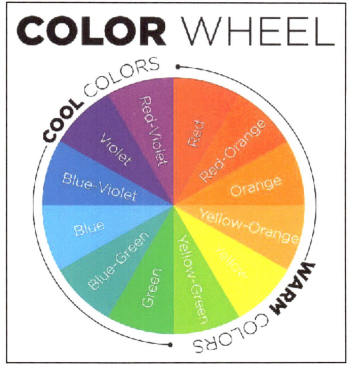

THE 3 PRINCIPALS OF COLOR!

Before we dive a little more into Color, I want to talk about the 3 Principal's of Color, Primary, Secondary and Tertiary. These are considered the 3 main principal's because they are ultimately the color's that you will create new color's from. These color's are also the color's used to create different color schemes, color contrasts and more.

Of all elements of design, you will find that Color is often the most challenging to work with or sometimes to even comprehend. Working with these principal's will help you better understand Color and the role it plays. Color can encompass such a broad spectrum that you can easily get lost in one color combination to another.

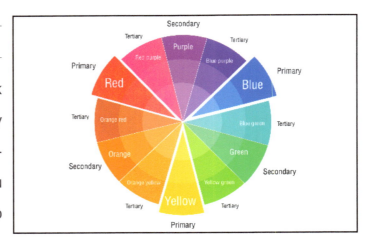

One thing that helps to remember is that Color creates emotional feeling's; meaning that when we see certain color's we are attracted to, they can invoke emotions.

If we know what color's we can use to mix and match perfectly, it is easier to apply these basic principal's. These principal's were created so you could have an easy theory of how to work with Color. Broken down for a more easily understood concept, the Color Wheel provides you with plenty of options to choose from. Focus on learning all you can about color theory and these main 3 principals.

If you are not to sure what Color Theory is, it's a body of practical guidance to color mixing and the visual effects of a color combination created from one of the 3 main principals of Color, mainly with primary colors. Using these principal's allows us to create visual interpretations with different color combos that offer's varying experiences for the viewer. You want to make this experience as pleasant as possible. ▶

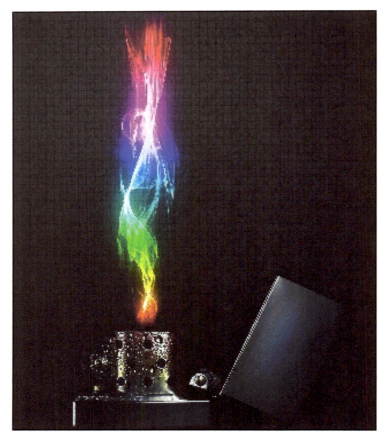

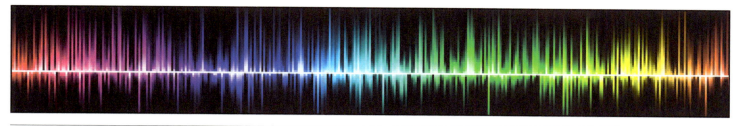

APPLYING THESE PRINCIPALS!

Understanding these principals can take you a long way. Take for example the picture to the left and above. With the ability of color blending, you have an exceptional display of graphics and color. Using the right mixture of colors can give off that visual interpretation you are looking for.

All three of these Principles are fairly easy to learn, and we will discuss them a little more in detail, but focus on using these to create good color combinations. With good combination's can come good chemistry.

THE CONFORMITY OF COLOR!

There are a few more things that are more important then Color, but ultimately it comes down to Color. A Color that can invoke one reaction in one person may invoke the opposite reaction in another, causing compromise within your design. Your goal is to try and please everyone, but compromise will definitely come into play.

There are many ways to add the emphasis of Color to your design, but you want to focus on what works best for you too many color's can easily offset your design, while using the right amount of color can add depth and interest to your composition. ▶

COLOR THEORY EXPLAINED!

Color Theories ultimately create a logical structure for your color. When it comes to Color Theory, there are three basic categories of Color Theory to remember; The Color Wheel, Color Harmony, and the Context of how your colors are used in your design.

You use these three Color Theory categories to develop color options and definitions. Color theory helps us explain how we perceive color; ultimately how colors mix and match. ▶

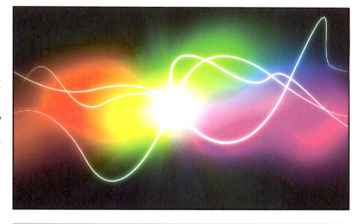

A lot goes into the choice of Color because there is so many color's to contend with. It is often said that color represent's certain feelings when we see it, so Color's can often give off feelings of warmth, excitement, happiness, calmness, energy and passion just to name a few, so learn to mix and match. ▶

PRINCIPLE OF PRIMARY COLORS!

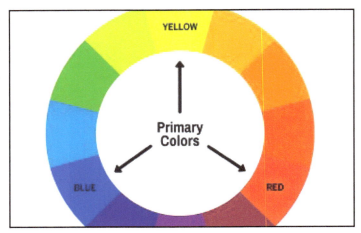

When it comes to Color Schemes and Color Theory nothing play's more of a role then the Color Wheel. The Color Wheel is ultimately where you develop your color theories, but ultimately develop your sense of color. Using the right balance of color's allows you to know which colors mix and match, but also which colors clash when combined together.

The basic principle of the Color Wheel starts with three primary colors – red, yellow and blue. These colors are considered to be Primary Colors because they are placed adjacent on the wheel from one another. Primary colors are the basis for all other color and any color can be made using a combination of primary colors.

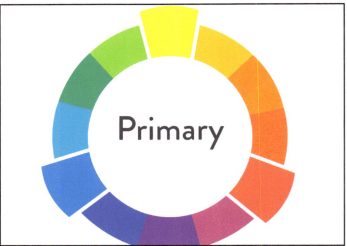

Primary colors also can not be mixed from other colors on the Color Wheel. They are the source of all other colors, and all color options are developed off them.

Mixing and matching is about creating the perfect color combination with the help of these primary colors. We've previously talked about the different color schemes you can develop. These color schemes are of course; complementary colors, analogous colors and monochromatic colors. Primary Color's are the top color's in any hierarchy or structure, seeing that your Primary Color's are considered to be the root of all other color's. Although color is never an exact science, you have the ability to develop color schemes that are pleasing and easy to comprehend. ▶

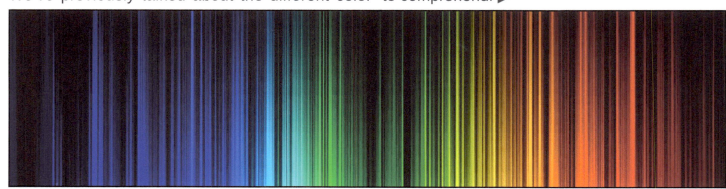

MIXING & MATCHING PRIMARIES!

Remember that no other color can be created or mixed without the help of your Primary Color's. Don't be alarmed though because as you see with the image to the left, mixing and matching the right Primary color's can provide you an abundance of color schemes and options.

Think of Primary Color's as the parents to your color because without them you are technically lost, but with them you can easily find your way. Color can be a tricky thing when you are trying to find the right match because it's easier for colors to clash with each other then to mix.

Look at other designs when you are thinking about color. Also one good thing to look at is the available Color Theory Poster, which can be found everywhere online. Remember with colors you can set mood's, attract attention, or simply make a statement.

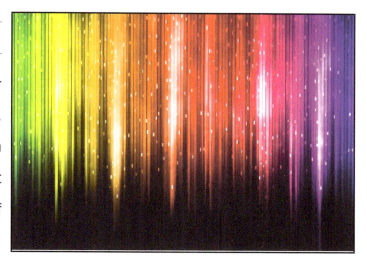

By selecting the right color scheme, you can create a pleasant experience for your viewer. Color can be your most powerful design element tool if you learn to use it effectively and efficiently.

By selecting the right color scheme, you can create a pleasant experience for your viewer. Color can be your most powerful design element tool if you learn to use it effectively and efficiently. ▶

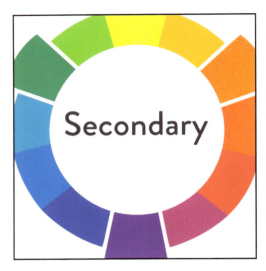
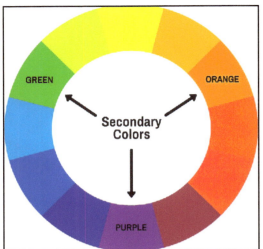

SECONDARY COLORS IN DESIGN!

Thinking of what we discussed about Primary Color's, Secondary Color's are like the kids of the bunch. These Color's are created by blending or mixing two Primary Color's in a given color. In color theory for designer's, the secondary colors are usually, green, orange, and purple, and are created by mixing two primary colors.

If you look at the example below you will see how this formula is created. With the simple addition of two Primary Color's, you are able to create a new mixture of color. The ratio of the primary colors you use when you mix them together will determine the final color hue of your secondary colors.

Color theory tells us that if we mix equal parts of two Primary Colors, we will create the colors of either green, orange, or purple, hence this is how they become our Secondary Color's.

This concept is the foundation for the Color Wheel and a lesson that is often taught in most Photoshop or Online Color classes. Depending on what type of Color Proportions you mix with your Primary Color's, will ultimately decide the ending Secondary Color.

For example, if you add more primary red than yellow to a red-yellow color mixture, you get a reddish orange tint, and vice versa, if you add more primary yellow than red, you get a yellowish orange tint. ▶

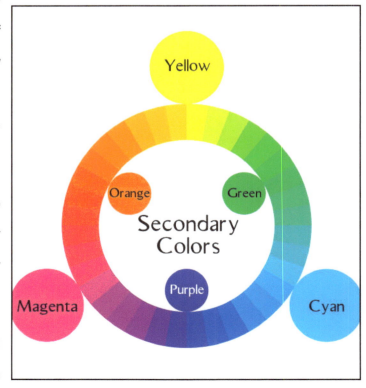

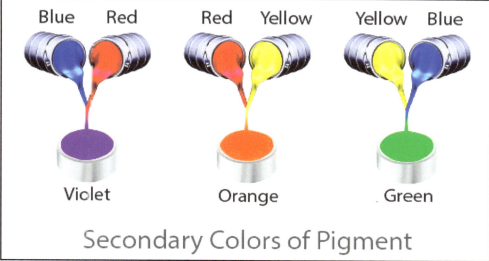

Blue   Red   Red   Yellow   Yellow   Blue

Violet   Orange   Green

Secondary Colors of Pigment

SECONDARY COLOR MIXTURE!

There is always a slight difference when it comes to Secondary Color's because of the two different forms of graphic design. If you are just designing for simple online print, where there is no original paper printing, or whether you are developing for original paper print. If you look at both examples provided, from the right to above, you can see the slight difference in color mixtures. In graphics you'll often see, orange, green and purple, but in the Print world you will often see, cyan, yellow and magenta.

Learn the difference between both color format's, because doing this will help you in your Color decisions. Since both color format's will provide you with an array of color combos and varieties, these colors can easily be manipulated to create a sense of balance and harmony. ▶

Always remember one color will always remain your prime base color, with the other two Secondary Colors playing the supportive role to this Primary Color. When you use the color mixtures wisely, you are able to mix and match all your primes to create the a broad spectrum of color's. ▶

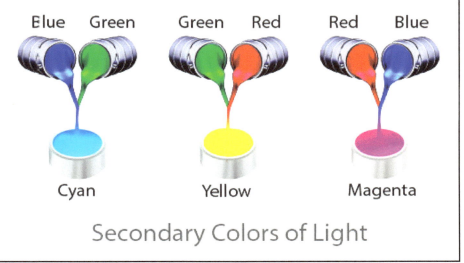

Blue   Green   Green   Red   Red   Blue

Cyan   Yellow   Magenta

Secondary Colors of Light

TERTIARY COLORS IN DESIGN!

The third type of color that we will discuss before we move on is Tertiary Color's. Tertiary colors are the resulting color formed when an equal amount of a primary and a secondary color are mixed. The primary and secondary color must be beside each other on the color wheel. For example, a mixture of 50 percent of the color red and 50 percent of the color magenta will result in the Tertiary Color of orange.

Since Tertiary Colors are combinations of your primary and secondary colors, there are a total of six Tertiary Colors; red-orange, yellow-orange, yellow-green, blue-green, blue-violet, and red-violet.

One of the easiest ways to create these colors is to take these color's and place the primary color before them. If you look at the list above, you will see that most of the six Tertiary Color's start with a Primary Color, then go into a secondary color. This is because with the right mixture of your Primary and Secondary Colors, whether it is 50/50, 75/25, 25/75, you are still using the saturation of each of these color's to create your Tertiary Color.

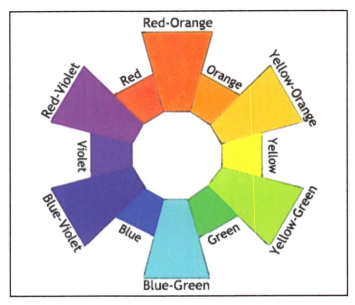

The structure of this color can easily come into play when you are choosing your Prime Color. As Secondary Color's are often referred to as the kids to Primary Color's your Tertiary Color's are considered the grandchildren of your Primary Color's.

You are creating this formality because for Tertiary Color's you are taking one Primary Color, and a Secondary Color that is right next to or nearest to your Primary Color. Using this process you are left with a color somewhere in between the two, creating your Tertiary Color Scheme.

You'll often see Artist's use Tertiary Color's because with them they are able to express complexity. Since these color's are often thought of as attractive, energetic and passionate, they can easily be used to create visual appeal and interest. Learn the use and properties of Tertiary Color's too create appeal because they can give off a different complexity. ▶

PERFECT BLEND OF CONTRAST!

We've referred to Color Contrast and it comes into play with Tertiary Color's too. Most Tertiary Co or's will often be referred to as lighter color's because of the sense they give off, this is accomplished in Contrast also with the mix of shades, tones and tints.

Unlike Color Contrast you are working with more directional and focused color's, therefore you are creating a sense of focus using a variety of color s. Since these color's are often seen as soft, subtle and comfortable color's, they give of an sense of harmony. As you can see in the examples provide, using the mixture of the right color can give your design emphasis and create a sense of interest.

Your goal is to easily create this interest without their being any confusion to your design, but working with these color's can ne tricky.

Since these color's are often used to draw in the concentration of your viewer, you can easily do this by providing them with appealing and pleasant color's to view.

You can often think of Spring color's when you are thinking of tertiary color's because you are working with color's that are often represented as soft and comfortable color's that help's the viewer concentrate more on the design. Take these two bottom image examples and you can see the color combinations I am referring too. ▶

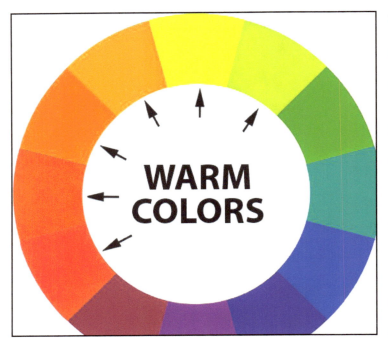

WARM COLORS IN DESIGN!

Although there are many theories of color out their, designer's usually tend to stick with our Color Theories of Warm and Cool Color's. This difference allows us to distinguish between light and dark colors or light and dark backgrounds.

Warm Color's tend to give off that comfortable feeling because they invoke a sense of warmth and positivity. Since these Color's usually originate from the primary source of Red, Yellow or Orange, they often give off a sense of passion and harmony.

For example think of elements like the sun and fire. These elements often give off a sense of warmth because they are inspirational to us. We see these elements as inspirational pieces in our daily lives because they give us that normalcy. The sun ultimately gives us life and existence, while fire is provided to enhance our way of living.

Without one another you have no harmonial balance in your life, therefore no control over what is perceived.

Perception gives direction, and with the right Color's you can conceive that perception to make your designs more investing to your potential reader's.

The phrase Warm Color's simply refers to color's that are used to describe any color that is vivid or bold in nature, such as the sun or fire.

I am sure we have all see Volcano's, and we can use this as an example. The glow of the flowing lava gives off a illusion of firery orange because the lava is basically on fire and the flow creates this glow, that we've all come to love. ▶

THE ATTRACTION OF WARM COLORS!

Somehow we all love burning fire, and fire added to a design creates a general interest of appeal. The same can be said when you are working with Warm Color's.

We love Warm Color's because they provide us with a feeling of coziness and warmth, this can be seen in our daily lives just by looking at the color of our house walls.

Our house walls often represent color's of appeal and comfort. This is because when we are at home we want to feel as comfortable as possible, with no distraction's, but simple relaxation.

You can use this philosophy when it comes to Warm Color's because these color's often give off these emotional feeling's. Keep in mind attraction equals appeal and vice versa, so it's your job to use color's that easily blend and contrast with each other, but keep that sense of comfort and warmth.

Of course when working with any color, it can be overwhelming, but just remember to focus on using the right color schemes and patterns to develop the right color mixes and matches. Since we live in color it is not to hard to find the right color matches for pleasant color combinations.

Your ability to learn how to use the Color Wheel will help you with this tremendously because it's easier to go off your primary color's and then start to blend the color's together to create Warmer Color's to use for your design's. ▶

A BALANCE OF COMFORT!

With the use of Red, Yellow and Orange you are creating an array of color and color varieties that offer a sense of warmth and comfort. These color's can be used to create some amazing artwork and show contrast in bland designs. Take a look at these images for example. The one to the right shows an excellent view of how warm color's compare to cool color's and how they show how you can use lighter color's to create a better sense of balance.

The harmony of these color's is what gives us that comforting feel because most of these color's remind of us nature and some of our natural surrounding's. Think of this when you are working with Warm Color's and you can find the right mixtures to use and combine.

Since we typically see these color's on a daily basis, you can often use these color's when you are thinking of what you are trying to achieve. ▶

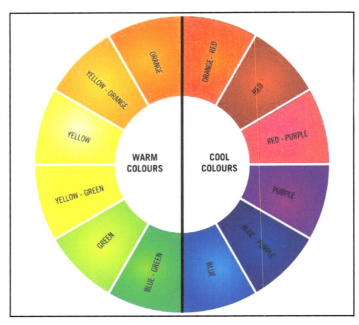

CONTRAST OF SPACE!

With the use of the mixture of color's using these Red's, Yellow's and Oranges you can easily create the element of space. What I am referencing is Space UP THERE, and not actual space In a design. For example, take the look at the image below, here you have a beautiful picture of space and what kind of color array's it can cast. ▶

NATURAL USE OF COLORS!

There beauty in the eye of the beholder, or so they say. Think of that when you are thinking of Warm Color's. Think of nature and your natural environment's. These will ultimately be your direction. ▶

STUDY WARM COLOR CHARTS!

Get familiar with Warm Color Chart's because they will help you come up with color ideas. Since they are easy to understand and easy to comprehend, you can use these to your advantage. ▶

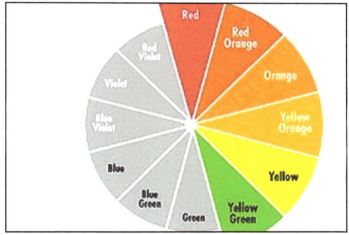

WARMTH OF THE SUN!

Prime examples of the use of Warm Color's are images of the sun and sunrises. These images create a sense of warmth and comfort, and because of this they are often designed with Warm Color's. ▶

COOL COLORS

COOL COLORS IN DESIGN!

The other Color Theory that designer's use mostly is Cool Color's such as blue, green, and purple . They are considered Cool Color's because they invoke a cool feeling usually reminding us of things like water and grass. These color's are often thought of because they can also give off the feeling of ice, cold and darkness.

Since Warm Color's often give off a sense of warmth and heat, Cool Color's will give off a sense of calmness and soothing. Cool colors make you feel calm, relaxed and refreshed because they often remind us of elements like water, ice and snow. These images usually give of a sense of calmness and used as wallpaper's and desktop screen saver's. Since they tend to put us in that meditation state, you will typically see them on computer screens or as downloaded wallpaper's floating around computer screens.

Water and snow usually gives us a feel of serenity, so it's only right that they are considered Cool Color's.

One plus about Cool Color's is that they give off a bigger sense of receding, meaning that even though the color option you may be using is small, the Color you choose itself recede's.

This theory is often used by home interior decorator's that are trying to make small room seem larger then it is. With Cool Color's they are able to create this contrast because Cool Color's recede, and can give off that sense of a larger element.

if they want a small room to seem visually bigger, they will use a Cool Color, this allows them to create the sense of a larger space. You can use this same method when it comes to Design, because you can use these Color's to create depth. ▶

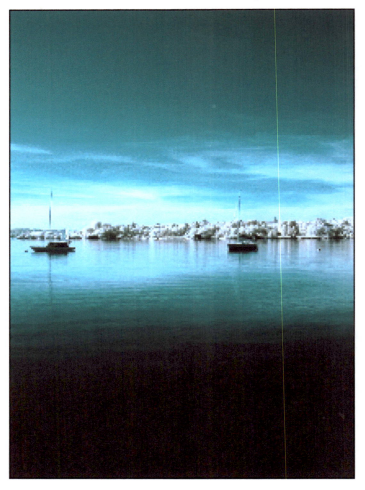

CALMNESS EQUALS SERENITY!

Cool Color's are used to describe any color that is calm or soothing in nature. The blues of the sky. Cool colors are not overpowering and tend to recede in space, therefore adding more emphasis then there actually is. Since there is a calmness with the Color's you are able to provide a composition that seems cool, functional and calm.

Think of it as the last time you got lost just looking at the blue sky, or sitting and enjoying the breeze coming off a lake. These experiences bring us a feeling of calmness and relaxation, a sooth ng experience where we can just sit back and relax.

Since the world is filled with non-stop act on in our daily lives, it's good to be able to take a break every now and then and sit and enjoy our surrounding's. Our lives are sometimes a daily struggle between stress and relief, it's good to just relax and take the time to enjoy some peace and serenity.

Cool Color's are often used to represent amazing waterfall's, ocean's and lake views because we find ourselves easily attracted to these images and scenery's. They often give off certain appeal and we find ourselves dreaming of being there instead of where we really are.

Use this calmness of serenity to attract your viewer's attention and you will be able to easily draw there eyes in. This is often referenced when you are designing from a center point because you are trying to find the best element's to balance together so you can create this serenity. ▶

SOOTHING OF WATERFALLS!

Since Cool Color's often remind us of cold and dark color's they can be sometimes referred to by looking at Waterfall's. The coolness of the flowing water, but also the darkness of the unknown bottom's. ▶

NATURAL USE OF COLORS!

Cool Color's also can be seen in our daily lives, just simply by looking at nature. Since they give off a natural sense of balance, you can use examples of landscapes and icy images to convey calmness and serenity. ▶

STUDY COOL COLOR CHARTS!

Get familiar with Cool Color Chart's because they will help you come up with color ideas. Since they are easy to understand and easy to comprehend, you can use these to your advantage. ▶

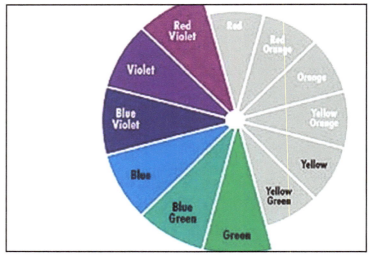

A BALANCE OF COMFORT!

Remember that Color can play a lot with our emotions because we see and perceive in Color. Since we can be emotionally attached to Color's, it is best to try and focus on using the right blend and mixtures of Color.

Also remember to use soothing Color's, for example check out these two images provided here. They represent a sense of calmness and comfort because they are displayed in a way that gives you that sense of relaxation. ▶

A BALANCE OF COOL COLOR!

Cool Color's can go along way with you because they are often used with sky and lake design's. Focus on looking at these design's to get ideas for using the right color mixtures to create appeal and interest.

Also remember to look at color wheel's and color examples to get a better sense of color range and color combination's. For example the image to the right gives you a perfect example of color options to choose. Since the color's are often started from your Primary, you can see how the color's can mix. ▶

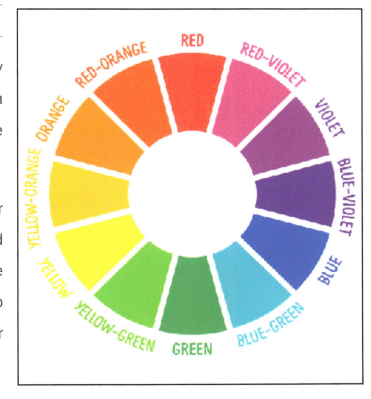

PHOTOSHOP Is a very important key program for any designer to have. It is one of the main design program's where you can do anything you can possibly think of. Used for just about everything from photo editing and enhancing to full creation of designs. Adobe has also provided numerous design programs for you. The best thing to do if you want to experience the use of all of them is to get their Creative Cloud Package. This usually runs about $10.00 a month or about $120 for the year. Unfortunately you can no longer just download the programs themselves, but this way does provide a cheaper way of using Adobe Creative Programs.

LEARN THE BASICS FIRST!

The concept is simple, yet so many people skip this first step and end up getting lost in a process they no longer understand. There are so many elements that can go into a simple design that it is good to have a head start. So learn the basic's because it will help you in the long run, but it will also help you understand more about techniques and tools.

Photoshop is a fundamental design tool that never stops changing and new tools and techniques are being developed by designer's and artist's daily. You can view these by simply going online and checking out the latest in Photoshop lessons and tutorials. These tutorial's are awesome for you to learn and they give you step by step process of how to do it right.

With this aptitude of knowledge you are able to better understand what Photoshop and it's capabilities is all about. Photoshop can be used to create just about anything you can think of, from simple print product's, to advanced web site layout's, to T-shirt' designs, but it's up to you to learn what your capabilities are and how you can improve them.

One thing to consider is that Photoshop is used by some of the top media and music companies today. Also note that most of today's newspaper companies, whether they are an online or offline publication, use Photoshop for layout and image enhancement. ▶

LEARN PHOTOSHOP YOUR WAY!

As discussed it is a good train of thought to learn Photoshop your way and focus on what you do best. If you are good at photo-editing and image manipulation, perfect that and vice versa for the design process. Stick to that theory and you will accomplish great things.

One great thing about Photoshop is that they allow you to Learn and develop at your pace. The lessons and tutorial's you can learn from are available 24/7, so you are never harbored to learning new techniques at your pace. As in the old word's, practice makes perfect, and working with Photoshop on a daily basis can deeply enhance your understanding of different principles and techniques.

With this ability you will be able to learn how to create and manipulate your concepts and ideas in a variety of ways. The elements to a good design is to have that design look and feel the way you want t to when it is first seen.

Since our eyes are instantly attracted to Color, knowing how to apply the right balance, keep's your design functional and interesting.

With dedicated lessons and tutorial's, you can learn about the many way's there is to help you with your designs. Learning Photoshop provides you with new knowledge and enhances a whole new world of creativity. Since there are so many thing's that goes into designing, knowing Photoshop and it's capabilities, allows you to think before you react.

A lot of times ideas and concept's in your head seem great, but they are just that, great concept's in your head and not on paper. With alignment, repetition, balance, contrast, hierarchy and the power of color hanging in the balance, it's good to know what tools you have at your disposal.

Turning nothing into something, is not necessarily easy, but with the help of Photoshop, the job is cut in half. Photoshop now makes it easier then ever to complete simple tasks such as: editing and enhancing photos, photo manipulation, illustrating, color mixing and much more. ▶

PAINTING YOUR PORTRAIT!

When your working with Photoshop, you can think of it as creating a painting. Photoshop provides you with the canvas, but it's up to you to create your masterpiece. So knowing what you can and can't do can go a long way. Photoshop is developed and built on a platform for the beginner designer's. It gives you the ability to learn what you can create and gives you tutorial's to learn what you can't.

One thing you will realize when you are designing and learning with Photoshop, is that the design and elements soon fall into place, which makes picking up new ideas come easy.

Since you are trying to create your masterpiece, it's a step-by-step process of planning, developing and creating. With Photoshop, you are able to work at your pace and design at your pace because the design process can take longer then expected. Don't be alarmed though, once you learn a new concept, after time, it becomes easier to do.

As I stated a little before, Photoshop is your canvas, and with plenty of tools, layer and effects to work with, you can easily create a masterpiece that will be enjoyed by your viewer's. Use other's to inspire you also because great minds think alike. ▶

PHOTOSHOP MAKES IT EASY!

One thing I love about Photoshop, is that they make it easier for you to learn about new elements and techniques. Since the design world is ever expanding you have the ability to stay up to date with the latest editions of tools and elements. This helps you become a better designer, because you are learning the tools of the trade.

You are never limited to what you can do, for example take a look around this book, because a lot of these images were created with Photoshop. So Photoshop allows you to create anything you can imagine. We discussed how important imagination is in the Creative Mind, so Photoshop goes hand in hand with the concept of being creative and Imaginative.

With a bevy of tools provided you can easily figure out how to edit, manipulate, create and blend new elements into your designs, so they create more depth and interest.

It's you ultimate goal to create an interesting art piece that attracts your viewer, but also appeals to the viewer. If you have no interest or appeal, you really have no functionality in your design. Therefore causing your viewer to be confused and easily put off, and not interested at all.

You definitely as a designer do not want this, so your goal is to use Photoshop to your advantage when you are trying to create cool and appealing designs.

With the ability to cross-train, learn tutorial's or study lessons, Photoshop provides you plenty of options to make your life a little easier. Design is a balance of give and take, it's good to know the capabilities of what certain Photoshop elements can do and what effects are at your disposal. ▶

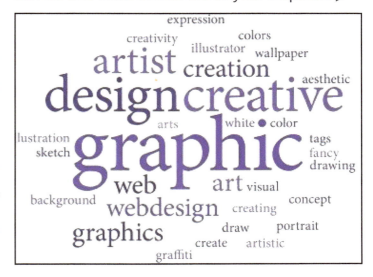

TUTORIALS & LESSONS THAT HELP!

Photoshop is such a powerful yet intuitive tool that can help you bring out the best in your design's, so if you are a serious designer or photographer, it is essential that you learn how to edit, manipulate, apply filter's and effect's to font's and images with Photoshop. Not only will this help you in the long run, but it will help you easily learn new tricks and techniques because you are well informed.

You can do this by easily studying and learning different techniques to image editing and manipulation, plus font and typography editing. One thing that I can never say enough is, Learn what your capabilities are and it will help you along the way. The same goes here, Photoshop has many tutorials and lessons out there for different editing techniques, so use them.

Photo editing, typography and font manipulation have come a long way since the old day's of using Corel Draw or Quark Express. Even though Corel Draw has definitely stepped up there game in the design world, Quark Express fell off. If you are not to sure what Corel Draw is, feel free to look up the design program, because you might find this program handy. Think of it this way, most design or print shop's today use Corel Draw instead of Indesign to complete stationary print projects.

Corel Draw is another excellent design program, because it not only gives you Corel Draw, but it also gives you Corel Paint, which is a cool editing program that Corel built to edit and manipulate photos and images. Although I stick to Photoshop as my premier design program, Corel Draw isn't bad to know or learn about. ▶

DEPTH OF PERCEPTION!

Many designer's often use Photoshop to create depth in their images. This gives off a visual perception of a balanced design and it's elements. You'll often see this in landscape or beach images. ▶

VISUAL INTERPRETATION & APPEAL!

As in imagination, you are not stuck to the certain stigma of design. You can take anything you can imagine and apply it to create a visual representation or interpretation of what you are thinking. ▶

EXPANDING YOUR HORIZONS!

There is never a limit to what you can imagine, and with Photoshop you can take this theory and apply to any design you see fit. You are the designer, you are able to imagine what you wan and simply apply Photoshop to create it. ▶

COLOR FOR ENHANCEMENT!

Another plus about the use of Photoshop is the ability to edit and manipulate color in your images. With this ability your able to draw out certain elements that can stand out and help create a center point to your design. This is of course known as your Focal Point, but with Photoshop it makes it easier to help your elements stand out, with the simple addition of color enhancement and effects. ▶

PHOTO EDITING & MANIPULATION!

Photoshop's speciality is Photo editing and manipulating. This is the main program used for designer's and companies all around the world for photo editing, whether it comes to magazine or just simple design pieces.

Since it's one of the easiest tools to work with, lead designer's will often focus on the use of Photoshop for photo shoots. It's a simple process when it comes to images, because image or photo editing encompasses the processes of altering images and photos, whether they are digital photographs, traditional photos, photo rendering's or illustrations.

Since it's a constant battle with finding the right image and photo to use, once you do, Photoshop makes it easy for you to edit it the way you see fit. With Photoshop you can easily use different elements to enhance and colorize your images. This gives your design more emphasis and visual appeal, allowing your design to have more depth and interest.

The awesome ability to enhance and edit photos helps you bring out the best in your photos just by simply applying these fundamental image-editing techniques. Color's can do some amazing things when you add them to your images.

There are many image editing tools and program's out there, for example, Photoshop, Corel Draw and Illustrator, but most designer's and photographers typically start out with Photoshop for basic editing because it is such a powerful tool and image manipulator. Photoshop's capabilities are like no other design program out there and can do what most other's can't. Photoshop also gives you this ability by providing an array of different elements, effects and tools to use. With the help of layer's, special effects and filter panel's, you are easily able to manipulate any image you want to. ▶

ENHANCING YOUR IMAGES!

Images are always going to come into play when you are creating or designing. Because of this fact it is good to learn everything you can about image editing so you can easily use Photoshop tools to do what you need to do.

There is a tremendous amount of equations that can go into enhancing your image, you want to focus on using the right tools to get the job done. Think of it this way, when you are editing an image you have to take into consideration, whether you are trying to add intensity, color, adding text, adding layers, enhancing, retouching, or just adding dimension, you'll see that a lot of equations goes into your design process.

You will also take into consideration whether you are applying filter's and effects to your images for enhancement. You can easily add photo effects with the use of different customizing elements provided by Photoshop to provide emphasis in your designs. For example, take these images above and to the right, they offer a sense of balance, but they were edited in a way to give off appeal and interest. Most wall art will often resemble a similar contrast because they are created to add the illusion of appeal.

Editing often depends on your purpose for the image, whether you are retouching photos or enhancing them. This is most important process for editing because each image used has it's own purpose.

Photo retouching, for example is mainly used for model's, fashion mags, wedding photography, removing spots and acne, removing blemishes, but can also be removing something as simple as wrinkles.

Photo enhancing on the other hand can be used to add different aspects to your design, ultimately to create emphasis. Here you will use different and opposite elements such as: size, type, balance, layers, color's, object's and shapes to create certain enhancements in your image. ▶

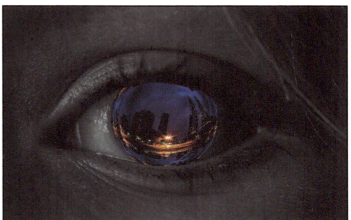

Photoshop is an incredible design tool to help you add visual interpretation and intensity to a very bland design. Since our goal is to create pleasing material for our viewer's, adding depth to a bland design can help draw in your viewer's eyes with the simple use of key focal points. ▶

**OLOR**. When doesn't color play a pivotal role in the process of design, I'd say never. The same process that we take define the color's we use is the same in Photoshop as it is anywhere else. The good thing about Photoshop is that they provide you with an array of color's to work with. In Photoshop you are not just working with the Color Wheel as we previously learned about, with Photoshop you are working with an array of up to 256 Color's, this all depends on 8 bit to 32 bit files (images). With this exceptional offer of value, you have a multitude of different color's at your disposal.

COLOR MODE OR IMAGE MODE!

Think of Modules when you are working with Color in Photoshop because instead of just primarily working off The Color Wheel, you will be designing with a different method.

If you think of your Color's as Color Modules, you will take a different approach working with color. You'll often see Photoshop reference them as Color Modes or Image Modes. The Color Mode, or Image Mode, simply determines how the components of your color are combined, based on the number of color channels in the available color model.

Photoshop uses these Color modes because they have an indexed Color Table that has stored, these 256 Color Array's. These Color Modes are usually Grayscale, RGB and CMYK. Color modes RGB & CMYK are the two most often used Color Modes in design. ▶

THE POWER OF COLOR!

Color can be a beneficial tool for you to use, because it provides so much that it can easily change a regular image to a colorful image.

For example take a look at these top two images and you will see the difference between a regular image and an enhanced image with Color. The colorful image stands out more, because you added depth to it, becoming more appealing to the eyes.

Working with Color Modes is a little different because you are working with Values Of Intensity within a pixelated image.

What I mean by this is that in each pixel of your image, (images are made of tiny little pixel's) the Color Mode chosen will have an color intensity value to it, depending on the component's in that color.

For example if your working with RGB Co or Mode the intensity Values will range from 0 (black) to 255 (white) for each of the components in the image, but

it is different with the CMYK Color Mode. In the CMYK Color Mode each pixel in your image is assigned a percentage value instead of an intensity value. For example, a primary Red color might contain 0% cyan, 99% magenta, 100% yellow, and 0% black. While a primary Blue may look something like 87% cyan, 76% magenta, 0% yellow and 0% black. In the CMYK Color Modes images of pure white are created when all four percentages have values of 0%. ▶

GRAYSCALE AND ITS COLOR USE!

When it comes to Grayscale, it uses the ability of both RGB & CMYK Color Modes, because Grayscale Color Image Mode uses different shades of gray from these color's. Working in Grayscale you are working with certain shades and tones to add depth to your design's. Certain darker color's offset the lighter color's but keep's the image balanced.

In 8-bit images, there can be up to 256 shades of gray. Every pixel of a Grayscale image has a brightness value ranging from 0 (black) to 255 (white). 0 (black) to 255 (white), but the values can also be measured as percentages of black, 0% is equal to white, 100% to black.

It really depend's on the image you are working with, obviously with 16 and 32-bit images the number of shades is greater then 8-bit images because of the bigger size. One easy way to remember about working in Grayscale Color Image Mode, is that Grayscale images only use black, white and shades of grays to define it's color's.

Whether you are working with color intensity values or color percentage values, it comes down to the values of black, white and shades of gray. Photoshop also allows you the ability to add depth to your Grayscale images with the help of shadows and highlights that you can manipulate. ▶

PHOTOSHOP GRAY SCALE MODES!

Photoshop gives you the ability to work with Grayscale in several different ways and because of this, it makes it easier to judge shades and tones of your images.

You can work in Grayscale Color Image mode, you can use your image adjustment level's or you can apply what we have learned about earlier, hues and saturation to Grayscale your images and increase the depth by adding shades, tones and tint's.

USING RGB COLOR MODES!

The RGB Color model is an additive color model in which red, green and blue are added together in various ways to produce a broad array of colors. It is named the RGB Color model because it comes from the initials of the three primary colors used, red, green, and blue.

These color's combined are what creates your color in RGB mode. As we previously discussed, RGB Color mode deals with intensity values. These values often range from 0 (black) to 255 (white) for each of the components or pixel's in the image.

Each Primary Color will have it's own level and each color can range from 0 to 100 percent of full intensity. With using red, green, and blue you can combine an array of color proportions to obtain any color in the visible COLOR spectrum.

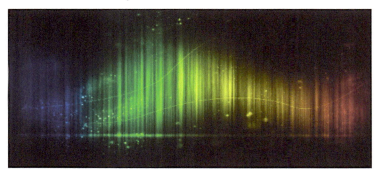

Since these are often considered your Primary Color's, you will base the color's you create off of each of these. The great thing about using RGB as a Color Mode, is that you have the ability to create and mix with the simple sue of slider's.

Since you are dealing with intensity values, you can easily find the right color's to mix by using the provided color slider's for each of your primary color's. Since each intensity value will start at 0, you have the option of seeing what color's you can create. ▶

THE INTENSITY OF COLOR!

With the RGB Color Mode, you will be working with the values between the 256 color's available from Photoshop.

Although it say's there are 256, you will really only be working with the integer's between 0 to 255. As we previously discussed 0 is simply black and 255 is white and you are working within this range.

IN THE WORLD OF PRINT!

Print has come a long way since the old day's. In today's print shop's you simply create your design and send it either to the Ryobi or Accuriopress Print machines or zerox copier's.

Once set up on the display screen you can easily print out a sample. This is a far cry from the far away days of using cyan, magenta, yellow and black ink

Since their is a vast array of color's you can choose, you can figure out what color's mix and what color's don't. Think of this also when you are working with Color Contrast because you are also working with tints and shades of color.

Using your intensity values wisely can help you create that spectrum of color that can be relied upon when you need to find different color matches for different designs. Since no two design's are ever the same, color combos can always be relied upon and used again. ▶

plates to create print publications. You would use these cyan, magenta, yellow and black ink plates to create your color varieties for your print publications. Getting ink on you was a daily thing, and trust me, your clothes start to show your work. Now it is very simple and just a click away because you have print machines that will print just about any form of publication or print that you need too.

USING CMYK COLOR MODES!

The CMYK color model is a subtractive color model, used in color printing, and is also used to describe the printing process itself. CMYK refers to the four inks used in color printing which are: cyan, magenta, yellow, and black. There are several ways that the CMYK Color Mode is different from the RGB Color Mode. Knowing this difference will help you choose the right color's to go with when you are designing in different format's of print.

A simpler way to think about it is that RGB Color's are referred to the primary color's of light, while CMYK Color's are referred to the primary color's of pigment.

This is because when combined, the RGB light's creates white, while CMYK inks combined gives off the presence of black.

CMYK inks are mostly used in print because it makes it easier to develop ink color's based off of these four color's combined. You will also here CMYK described as the printing process itself because these are the four key color's used in any print pro-

duction. The main difference here is that you will be working in percentage values instead of intensity values. With RGB you use integer values, but with CMYK, your color scheme will look more like 0% cyan, 99% magenta, 100% yellow, and 0% black. You can see the difference in values that you will be using, but each percentage with represent a portion of color.

With Photoshop and other program's you no longer have to worry about using the right Color Mode. If you find the right color image mode to use and you like it, keep it. ▶

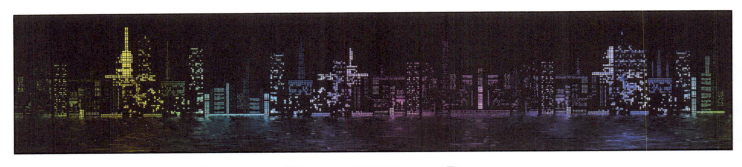

IMAGES
IN DESIGN!

Images is what makes your design stick out and stand out above the rest. Using the right image editing tools can easily enhance any design and make it more appealing!

IMAGES, can make or break your design and knowing which ones to use and which ones not too, can help you in the long run. When it comes to images, it can be just as tricky as picking the right color. You want your design to blend, but with images it's a matter of having the right balance. Images with no balance gives an offsetting feeling to your viewer and can easily cause confusion and disorganization.

This is typically used to create focal point's and point's of interest in your design's and creations.

We've talked about Center Point's and how they can be very effective because they help draw in your viewer's eyes to certain areas of the design, same process goes for images. Your using your images to create these center points so your viewer can easily understand the functionality of your design, this also makes it easier to comprehend your design.

Image placement can also play this role, because when you are using several images, one will tend to offset the other. ▶

FINDING IMAGES TO USE!

Images tend to be appealing drawing in your viewer, with this comes your responsibility to make sure that your viewer's are engaged to your design. With the help of images and image placement, you can create contrast between the images used and add balance to the rest of the design.

This is really the easy part of the design process because there is tons of images available out there. From stock photos available directly from Adobe, to stock photos available from just about any design source, you can always find the right images to use. Make sure to watch out for copyright laws because they can come into play with certain images.

Not all images that are copyrighted are unavailable, some come with certain restrictions and licenses for commercial use. If you see an image that you like and it is a wallpaper, but says copyrighted, click onto it to make sure that is the circumstances. Some images that say that they are, aren't actually copyrighted,

but the images on the page that come with the image, might be. It's really a matter of give and take because designer's are creating images everyday and some have restrictions and some don't. What I like to do to stay on the safe side is usually just enter FREE Wallpaper's in your google, bing or yahoo search bars. Doing so allows you to easily download available images and use them at your disposal for your design's.

Most if not all of the images available in this e-book came from FREE wallpaper searches, so you can see that you can easily download and use some awesome images. Of course if the image is your's, you undoubting have full copyrights to the image and other's have to ask you for the download. So be aware of where you can download images and where you can't. ▶

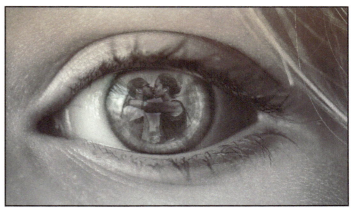

USING THE RIGHT IMAGES!

Now that you know that it's easy to find images to use, which ones do you use? This is ultimately up to you because you are the designer, so it's up to you which ones you think will work best with the concept of your design.

Since you know what direction you are trying to go with the design, you can easily decide on which images will give you this direction. Use images that add depth and interest to your design's because a bland design tends to be unappealing and very confusing to your viewer. Since we talked about the value of Perception, it can come in to play here, with the use of images and image placement. Use elements that appeal to your viewer's.

IMAGES ARE WHAT'S APPEALING!

Our eyes perceive where the design is trying to send us and if this direction is offset by the use of the wrong image or placement, your design can easily be ignored and looked over. You are not trying to aim for this goal because if your design's are off putting, it can be extremely hard to draw in your viewer's attention. You want to focus on using the right balance between element's so the viewer is easily entertained and interested in what you are offering.

Using the right images is what can be appealing to your viewer because it helps draw in their attention, then once drawn in they focus on what you are offering and what you are trying to get across. Appeal is the ultimate attraction, so make your's appealing. ▶

ELEMENTS AND IMAGE PLACEMENT!

2D and 3D design's can be very appealing by the use of several elements because it gives of that visual interpretation. It's easier to see and understand what you are trying to achieve then to try and look at a design to figure out what's going on. Element's within your image can play a huge role in visualization because it easily gives off depth.

if you look at the images provided on this page you can easily see that they are all created to add depth and interest to each design. Each artist's took the time to provide a clear sense of what they were trying to achieve and what they wanted to represent visually.

I chose these images because they give off a range of different concept's. Not one image is the same so you can see that no matter how you choose to lay your element's, placement is a very key necessity.

Image placement plays an important role in the process of design because to little can offset your image, but to much can cause confusion and dis-

tortion. Focus on the right image placement and using the space provided wisely. You have plenty of room to work with, so if you place your elements and images wisely, it creates a greater sense of balance.

Photoshop gives you a blank white canvas to start with, but you aren't necessarily stuck to this white background. Keep in mind white can give off a sense of unbalanced space, so a lot of designer's will generally use backgrounds or images that cover the whole canvas to reduce this space. ▶

DEPTH OF IMAGE PERCEPTION!

Understanding what appeals to the eyes and what doesn't isn't necessarily an easy task. Stay focused on your concept and improving it from their. Once you have a notion of what you are trying to accomplish, the pieces soon fall into place. Learn different Image placement theories and concept's, because they can save you time. ▶

USE OF GREAT BACKGROUNDS!

Great backgrounds for images can be found everywhere you can go online. From wallpaper backgrounds to desktop backgrounds, you will always find good use for these backgrounds. Once you find the right background, it's just a matter of choosing what elements you want to blend with your image. ▶

BLENDING IMAGES TOGETHER!

As designer's one thing we absolutely love is the use of being able to blend different elements together to create cool contrasted concepts that look awesome when combined together right. You are not limited to what you are able to combine, as long as the elements you choose; blend. If there is no blend to the elements you are using, there will be no sense of balance to your design. As you will see with the images on this page, each design has it's own element's that are used to create a sense of balance and focus. You can see that you are not limited with element's and there is a vast array of blends you can accomplish.

FINDING BALANCE WITH IMAGES!

Balance is very important in any design, as we previously discussed, but balance with images can come more into play then expected. You always want to find the right balance with images, this makes it easier to show the contrast of the different elements used.

For example the image above shows the classic car look, but add's the elements of a background and different color elements on the car. This helps draw in the viewer's attention by creating contrast between these elements. It's easy to see that the car is clearly the center point of the design, but it gives of appeal when you add different elements of attraction. Another example, staying with the car concept is the image below. Here is also a good example of different element use and how the elements in the image balance each other out. You are not limited to the elements you can use with your images, so don't be afraid to go outside the box. Mixing and blending the right element's can hugely affect the appeal to your design.

Another prime example of the right balance between elements is the image below of Posiedon. The designer was able to take create the perfect blend of elements to give off this cool rendition of the all mighty Posiedon. Prime examples of good symmetrical balance with blending are movie poster's. They use several elements to try and draw you in, once drawn in they use focal point's to peak your interest. Once interested it's just a matter of time before your checking movie times and to see when the movie comes out. ▶

IMAGE COLOR MANIPULATION!

One of the awesome things about working with Images in Photoshop is Image Color Manipulation. Look at the images on this page and you can see how Color Manipulation was used to enhance certain elements in each photo. Not only does this take a bland photo and make it pop more, but it also adds visual interest and appeal to your design.

It can be small manipulations to big manipulations, it's up to you to keep the balance between the elements and the image.

We've talked about Image Placement and the same concept can go into Color Manipulation, because you are trying to keep a sense of balance by adding contrast within your design to capture the viewer's eyes. Color is the ultimate decision maker because it plays such an important role in the design process.

Color can easily take your image from bland to exciting, with just the simple addition of blending a few color's into your elements. Since you have over 256 Color's to possibly mix and work with, Color will never be a limited option.

Focus on the right color blends because this will ultimately decide the role that the colors you are using will play. To make certain elements stand out from the rest, use the right Color Combo's to make sure that they are appealing to your viewer.

Color Contrast is key when you are trying to make your design's more appealing to your viewer's. Since Color is emotional, when we see colors we are attracted to, they give off perceptions, keep this in mind when using Color Manipulation. ▶

COLOR MAKES ANYTHING NICE!

You'll often see Color represented in Flower Design's, since flower's are always considered to be vibrant and lively. When trying to find the right Color Manipulation, take a look at examples like the one to the left. They offer you a good example of how Color's can be blended and mixed to create awesome design's. The same process goes for adding depth for visual intensity. Take a look at the image above and you will see that the designer was able to creatively blend the elements of fire and ice with Earth being the Center Point; to add intensity to the design.

VISUAL INTERPRETATION!

Many designer's often use Photoshop to create depth in their images. This gives off a more visual interpretation of a balanced design and it's elements. Color add's so much to simple designs, it's amazing. ▶

CALMNESS IS SERENITY!

Most design's will often give off a sense of serenity, because the designer took the time to find the right elements to use to create a sense of harmony between the elements. For example, you can see in the image to the left that the designer created a sense of serenity and balance between a beautiful young woman and a great white shark. Two element's that are not usually blended together; with the right mix of elements you can create amazing design's with visual appeal. ▶

BE ORIGINAL

Use **Color** and **Texture** to add *interest*

TWENTY ONE
AWESOME TIPS!

I want to finish this book out with 21 Awesome tips and strategies that will help you along the way. Check out some of these awesome tips and tricks, and use them to the best of you ability, trust me they will take you far!

[01] Open your mind to new tricks, techniques, information and knowledge and it will be greatly received in the end, taking you a long way. We learn new things every day, so why not harness this knowledge and use it to the best of your ability. Learn new techniques, but also perfect what you know and you will never go wrong in the end.

[02] Most people think that they are graphic designer's, unfortunately this is far and few between, and they are not. Sadly true, but they are sadly mistaken. If designing was easy, everyone in the world would be doing it. Some don't have the talent, but the ones that do can create some amazing things. Are Your One?

[03] Imagination and creativity can sometimes be more important than knowledge.
I know we always hear the saying knowledge is power, but so is imagination and creativity. Since all three can play a pivotal role in the process of design, who is to say which one has more sway.

[04] A Creative Mind at work is a very scary thing. it comes up with some imaginative design's.
Harness your creativity and observe other's when you are coming up with design's because you can come up with some crazy ideas and concept's.

[05] Use your Creative Mind to th nk of new way's and ideas to transform your designs into masterpieces with different element's.
Using your creative side is what Graphic Designing is all about. You are starting with nothing and creating it into something. This concept is just the start.

[016] Creative Thinking and critical thinking can play a valuable role in the process of design.
Creative thinking and critical thinking go hand in hand with the design process because both will help you focus on the direction you are trying to go.

[077] When thinking about the design in the creative process, always think outside the box.
Use your imagination when it comes to thinking about new concepts and ideas. Think outside the box and away from the norm.

[08] Learn the simple basics to Photoshop and Design and it will take you a long way.
Knowing and learning what you can and can't do, ultimately saves you time and effort. It's easier to work with what you know, then don't know.

[09] Learn what you know, perfect it and apply it to your designs.
Not every design comes easy, so knowing what you want to do is a great help. Perfect what you know and you will soon develop new techniques and trends.

[110] Learn how to be creative and energetic when it comes to your graphic designs.
The benefits of being creative are extremely beneficial because it allows you to try out new ideas and concepts, without having to be worried, whether if they will work or not.

[111] Learn Photoshop and the design process at your pace and study new techniques your way, on your time.
If the norm doesn't work for you, no worries, you need to learn your way. Doing this allows you to develop at your pace, not pushing to hard to soon, allowing you to actually learn what your doing.

[172] Use Photoshop examples, lessons and tutorials to your advantage.
There are tons of new tutorial's and lesson's available for you to learn from, but also new tutorials and lesson's are being created daily, so you'll never miss out.

[113] Online web sites are your greatest and best source for everything you will need.
Online is where you can basically find anything you need because they have an unlimited source of resources that is available 24/7.

[174] Photoshop provides you with an exceptional array of learning tools, resources and material.
One thing that is awesome about Photoshop is that you don't have to go anywhere to learn, you can learn directly right from their program. They offer a variety of tutorial's right from their program.

[115] Adobe Creative Cloud is a great service to use, but be aware because you don't need all the programs that are available.
Charging a monthly fee can be a pain, but that's really the only way Adobe let's us use their product's, but be aware of other program's that you don't necessarily use, and it might save you money.

[116] Photo's, Images, Font's, you will find online to be the greatest source for great images, font's and photos to use. .
There are plenty of stock photo options available online and most of these come free with a membership.

[174] Finding FREE images and photos to be able to easily use in your designs and compositions.
You can find lot's of free images and photos online from different web sites that provide free stock photo downloads or digital images.

18 Use Free Wallpaper's and Desktop Backgrounds in your design's.

Most wallpaper's are usually free with a simple download. Be aware that some may have copyright's so be sure to look before you use them. If they are copyrighted they usually block you from downloading or saving the image.

19 Copyrighted Images can easily kill your design if not used properly. Since these images are often found online, some designer's only want you to use them at there disposal.

Most wallpaper images and photos are usually free with a simple download, but make sure when you are downloading them the images that say for non-commercial use only are the ones you stay away from.

20 Use other graphic designer's design's as inspiration for your design's. Since there are many design's out their you can draw ideas from there concept's and design's.

There are some amazing design's out there and looking at them can give you some great ideas. Since the Creative Mind is always working and going, lean on this to get you ahead of the game.

21 It'll all work out in the end. Be patient and don't rush your design's or creative concept's. Balance them between the time you have and the time it will take you to complete the project.

Relax and don't rush greatness, because in time it all work's out. Take your time when you are creating your design's, patience is a virtue.

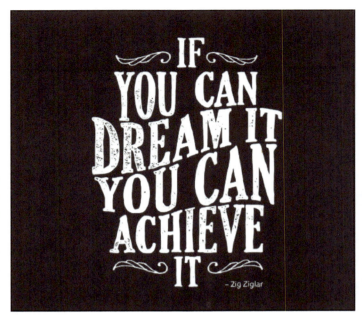

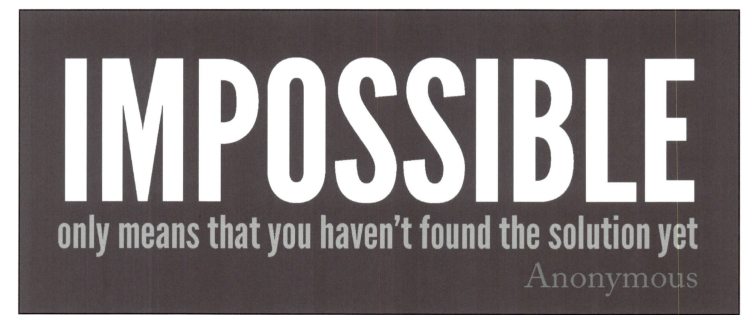

Let's finish it off with this beautiful picture. As in many design's any design can be elegant and stand out if done right. The perfect blends of images and color can go hand in hand with each other, but if you focus on working with the right elements, you will ultimately be able to create some amazing designs.

N THE END it ultimately comes down to you. If you learn the right techniques and method's, you can easily grow as a designer, and become an even better designer. Use what you have learned today and use it to your advantage because of course with knowledge comes power. Your power will just be in the form of being able to create amazing and interactive graphics that appeals to your viewer's. Learn these processes and method's and you can easily understand how to mix and match color, how to mix color elements with images, how to edit photo's, how to use the right image placement, what color's to use, what color modes can do what, what the color wheel is all about, what cause intensity and depth, and ultimately how the design process occurs.

THANK YOU FOR TAKING THE TIME!

Here I just want to finish it out by saying thank you for taking the time to learn with me. I hope this book will help you with the design process and ease your mind a little bit. Remember that you can never stop learning and developing new techniques and new color blends. Also don't forget to check out the Reference guide provided.

www.ingramcontent.com/pod-product-compliance
Lightning Source LLC
Chambersburg PA
CBHW041419050326

40689CB00002B/580